CITYSPOTS
STRASBOURG

Thomas Cook

NEATH PORT TALBOT

WHAT'S IN YOUR GUIDEBOOK?

Independent authors Impartial up-to-date information from our travel experts who meticulously source local knowledge.

Experience Thomas Cook's 165 years in the travel industry and guidebook publishing enriches every word with expertise you can trust.

Travel know-how Thomas Cook has thousands of staff working around the globe, all living and breathing travel.

Editors Travel-publishing professionals, pulling everything together to craft a perfect blend of words, pictures, maps and design.

You, the traveller We deliver a practical, no-nonsense approach to information, geared to how you really use it.

ABOUT THE AUTHOR

Based in the Black Forest, Germany, Kerry Walker is a freelance writer and contributes to numerous leading travel guides and publications. Kerry has authored some 15 travel books, including Thomas Cook CitySpots Vienna, Leipzig, Geneva and Cardiff. She regularly crosses the border to Strasbourg to brush up her French, eat *flammekueche* and stroll the banks of the River Ill.

CITYSPOTS
STRASBOURG

Kerry Walker

Thomas Cook

Written and updated by Kerry Walker

Published by Thomas Cook Publishing
A division of Thomas Cook Tour Operations Limited
Company registration No: 1450464 England
The Thomas Cook Business Park, 9 Coningsby Road
Peterborough PE3 8SB, United Kingdom
Email: books@thomascook.com, Tel: +44 (0)1733 416477
www.thomascookpublishing.com

Produced by The Content Works Ltd
Aston Court, Kingsmead Business Park, Frederick Place
High Wycombe, Bucks HP11 1LA
www.thecontentworks.com

Series design based on an original concept by Studio 183 Limited

ISBN: 978-1-84848-060-5

First edition © 2007 Thomas Cook Publishing
This second edition © 2009 Thomas Cook Publishing
Text © Thomas Cook Publishing
Maps © Thomas Cook Publishing/PCGraphics (UK) Limited
Transport map © Communicarta Limited

Series Editor: Lucy Armstrong
Production/DTP: Steven Collins

Printed and bound in Spain by GraphyCems

Cover photography (European Parliament Building) © Jon Arnold Images Ltd/Alamy

CONTENTS

INTRODUCING STRASBOURG

Introduction..............................8
When to go 10
Christmas in Strasbourg 14
History....................................16
Lifestyle..................................18
Culture....................................20

MAKING THE MOST OF STRASBOURG

Shopping.................................24
Eating & drinking 27
Entertainment
  & nightlife............................31
Sport & relaxation.................35
Accommodation 37
The best of Strasbourg 42
Suggested itineraries 44
Something for nothing 46
When it rains 48
On arrival................................50

THE CITY OF STRASBOURG

Grand Ile.................................60
Petite France...........................76
Krutenau &
  University District................90

OUT OF TOWN

Colmar...................................104
Saverne..................................116

PRACTICAL INFORMATION

Directory................................128
Emergencies 138

INDEX 140

MAPS

Strasbourg 52
Strasbourg
  transport map.....................56
Grand Ile................................62
Petite France...........................78
Krutenau &
  University District................92
Strasbourg region................106

SYMBOLS KEY

The following symbols are used throughout this book:

ⓐ address ⓣ telephone ⓦ website address ⓔ email
ⓛ opening times ⓝ public transport connections ⓘ important

The following symbols are used on the maps:

𝒊	information office		points of interest
✈	airport	O	city
✚	hospital	O	large town
🛡	police station	○	small town
🚍	bus station	=	motorway
🚆	railway station	—	main road
✝	cathedral	—	minor road
❶	numbers denote featured	—	railway
	cafés & restaurants		

Hotels and restaurants are graded by approximate price as follows:
£ budget price ££ mid-range price £££ expensive

Abbreviations used in addresses:

av.   avenue
blvd   boulevard
pl.   place (square)

◗ *Place Kléber lit at night*

INTRODUCING
Strasbourg

Introduction

Picture a labyrinthine old town squatting beneath an awe-inspiring Gothic cathedral, laced with canals and punctuated with cobbled squares, and you're dreaming of Strasbourg – a UNESCO World Heritage Site that grabs you from the first moment with its unspoilt beauty and laid-back village feel. Blending German down-to-earthiness with French finesse, this superlative city by the River Rhine has bounced across the border for centuries and the result is a heady cocktail of both countries.

Stepping from Grande Ile's knot of winding streets to Petite France's kaleidoscope palette of half-timbered houses hugging the banks of the River Ill, this is Alsace at its picture-book best. Despite its 450,000-strong population, this vibrant university city has preserved its charm. Whether you want to poke around markets brimming with local produce, sip fruity Sylvaner wines by the riverside or glimpse Goya masterpieces, you can graze for days on Strasbourg's riches.

And yet there's more to this city than meets the eye. Scratch the surface to find the crystalline EU Quarter where brains buzz, chichi boutiques and a growing crop of funky clubs in Krutenau that keep partygoers on the dance floor till dawn. Yep, the locals certainly know a thing or two about enjoying themselves – from Michelin flavours to crisp *flammekueche* on pavement cafés, cosy *winstubs* to cellars where beer flows freely. With acres of parkland to explore, nature is also never far away – a reminder that Strasbourg is a country kid at heart.

After a stint in the city, kick off your personal treasure hunt to discover the region's lesser-known gems, from vine-hopping along the picturesque Alsatian Wine Route to hiking the gently rolling Vosges mountains. Take a day trip to Saverne to climb precipitous castles and ramble through rose gardens, or head south to Colmar to boat through Little Venice and spy Bartholdi creations. Once upon a time there was Strasbourg, but that was just the beginning of Alsace's fairytale ...

⬧ *Strasbourg's Covered Bridges* (Ponts Couverts) *in the morning light*

When to go

SEASONS & CLIMATE

With a mild and pleasant climate, Strasbourg has year-round appeal. Summer brings dry, sunny weather hovering between 20°C and 30°C (68°F–86°F) – the time to come for open-air cafés humming with life, markets brimming with fresh produce and picnics in Parc de l'Orangerie. Autumn temperatures average 12°C (54°F), spelling fewer crowds and golden days in the city's plethora of parks and gardens.

Wrap up warm in winter for chilly days when temperatures sometimes drop below 0°C (32°F) and bring a dusting of snow. The streets aglow with thousands of tiny fairy lights, the scent of mulled wine at the Christmas market and an ice rink all add to the festive fun. Spring days are warm at 10°C–18°C (50°F–64°F), but pack a brolly for sudden showers. Nature lovers come to stroll the gardens in full bloom and go hiking in the nearby Vosges mountains.

ANNUAL EVENTS

January

Riesling du Monde Strasbourg is passionate about wine and proves it by hosting this contest to find the world's best Riesling. Some 230 tasting tables give wine lovers the chance to quaff dry, fruity whites. ⓐ Palais de la Congrès ⓣ 03 88 37 21 23 ⓦ www.riesling-du-monde.com

March

Giboulées de la Marionnette (Puppet Theatre Festival) French and international companies entertain kids of all ages by staging this fantastic puppet festival. ⓐ 7 rue des Balayeurs ⓣ 03 88 35 70 10 ⓦ www.theatre-jeune-public.com

March/April

Strasbourg Carnival The arrival of spring is carnival time. Expect plenty of fun-fuelled events from brass bands to late-night partying. The highlight is the costumed parade, a colourful affair of larger-than-life characters that weave their way through the city's streets. ⓣ 03 88 60 97 14 ⓦ www.strasbourg.fr

April

Festival des Artefacts See the next big thing play live at this new-wave music festival, where bands from across the globe pump up the volume with everything from punk to hard rock

◔ *There's nothing like a mug of hot chocolate to beat the chill*

and reggae. ❷ Parc des Expositions du Wacken ❶ 03 88 23 72 37
Ⓦ www.festival.artefact.org

May–September
Voix Romane Medieval melodies resound at this festival of early
music held in historic and religious settings along the pilgrims'
way, *Route Romane*. ❶ 03 90 41 02 02 Ⓦ www.voix-romane.com

June
Festival of Music Music buffs book tickets for this classical
festival, staging first-rate opera and concerts. ❶ 03 88 15 44 66
Ⓦ www.festival-strasbourg.com

July
Bastille Day Join the high-spirited locals to celebrate Bastille
Day on 14 July. The party features dancing, concerts and a huge
firework display in Petite France. Ⓦ www.strasbourg.fr

August
Street Entertainment Festival Heating up Strasbourg's summer
programme, this festival welcomes jugglers, clowns, acrobats,
musicians and mime artists to the city's streets and squares.
Ⓦ www.strasbourg.fr

September/October
Festival Musica Classical music with a contemporary twist hits
a high at this autumn festival. From experimental orchestral
performances to opera, this event brings top talent to the fore.
❶ 03 88 23 46 46 Ⓦ www.festival-musica.org

November

Jazz d'Or Sway to saxophone and blues rhythms at this lively event, where some of the world's best jazz musicians make an appearance. ☎ 03 88 36 30 48 ⓦ www.jazzdor.com

St'art Art lovers turn out in droves for this contemporary art fair, where galleries present a modern display of paintings and sculptures. ⓐ Parc des Expositions du Wacken ☎ 03 88 37 21 21 ⓦ www.st-art.fr

December

Christmas Market Whiffs of gingerbread and mulled wine, the twinkling of Christmas trees and sound of carol singers around Notre-Dame Cathedral make Strasbourg's festive market enchanting. ☎ 03 88 52 28 28 (tourist office) ⓦ www.noel-strasbourg.com

PUBLIC HOLIDAYS

These dates show the official public holidays in Alsace:

New Year's Day 1 Jan
Good Friday 10 Apr 2009; 2 Apr 2010; 22 Apr 2011
Easter Monday 13 Apr 2009; 5 Apr 2010; 25 Apr 2011
Labour Day 4 May 2009; 3 May 2010; 2 May 2011
Whit Monday 1 June 2009; 24 May 2010; 13 June 2011
All Saints' Day 1 Nov
Armistice Day 11 Nov
Christmas Day 25 Dec
Boxing Day 26 Dec

Christmas in Strasbourg

From late November to New Year's Eve, Strasbourg gets festive as the city's winding streets and cobbled squares are transformed into an Alsatian winter wonderland complete with glittering lights, the scent of cinnamon and carols echoing from the cathedral. As dusk sets in, decorated shop windows entice shoppers to loosen their purse strings and the 25 m (82 ft) tree on Place Kléber twinkles. If you're seeking Christmas spirit straight out of the picture books, *Noël* in this enchanting city won't disappoint.

The icing on the Christmas cake is the traditional *Christkindelsmärik* market held on Place Broglie and Rue de la Comédie dating back to 1570, which makes it one of the oldest in France. Here delicious gingerbread, hand-carved nativity figurines and steamy mulled wine are proof that Germany is but a pretzel-throw away. Stalls are piled high with wood-carved decorations, toys and local crafts that make unique gifts. Even if there's no room in your suitcase (or stocking), it's worth strolling the streets fanning out from Place de la Cathédrale to soak up the atmosphere.

Kids and kids at heart get their skates on to slide and twirl on Place du Château's open-air ice rink beside the illuminated Notre-Dame Cathedral, and glimpse Santa who makes regular appearances around the centre. Children also go wide-eyed at the abundance of sticky sweets, glowing nativity scenes, colourful street entertainers and the *contes d'hiver* (winter stories) told in the Chamber of Commerce and Industry's vaults on Place Gutenberg.

Culture reaches a high at Christmas. Book lovers should check out the Noël du Livre, where Strasbourg goes back to its literary roots with a festival dedicated to the written word, showcasing an impressive collection of book engravings and prints. Music buffs, too, are kept entertained at advent with a line-up of 50 concerts, where choirs, gospel singers, soloists and bands performing in churches across the city breathe seasonal cheer into Strasbourg. ☎ 03 88 52 28 28 (tourist office) ⓦ www.noel-strasbourg.com

🔺 *Christmas lights decorate the Strasbourg streets*

History

At the crossroads of European trade routes and strategically located on the River Rhine, Strasbourg has a long and colourful past that has seen it change hands several times between Germany and France – hence the reason why the bilingual locals speak both Alsatian (an Alemannic dialect of German) and French fluently. While many history books trace the city's origins back to Roman times, Strasbourg was actually inhabited long before by Celtic tribes who called it Argentorate. Artefacts on display in the Archaeological Museum support this claim.

Strasbourg made its mark on the map in 12 BC when the Romans set up camp on the banks of the Rhine and named their military outpost Argentoratum. This occupation lasted almost five centuries until the fall of the Roman Empire. During the fifth century, the town came under the rule of the Alamanni, Huns and Franks who gave it the name Stratisburgum, meaning 'the town of roads'. Over the centuries, Strasbourg prospered. Indeed, it was here that the famous Oath of Strasbourg was sworn in 842, providing one of the earliest examples of a Romance language other than Latin.

A period of unprecedented growth began in the Middle Ages when Strasbourg flourished to become a major trade hub. After a long and bitter struggle, the city finally managed to prise itself free from the ruling bishops in 1262 and was awarded the status of free imperial city. Fishermen, tanners and gardeners inhabited Petite France, the famous Covered Bridges were constructed and the almighty Notre-Dame Cathedral was built little by little. When it was completed in 1439 it became the world's tallest building, leaving the Great Pyramid of Giza in the shade.

Strasbourg and much of Alsace was seized by France in 1639 to prevent it from falling into the clutches of the Spanish. The 18th century culminated in the French Revolution and the downfall of the aristocracy. In 1792, Claude Joseph Rouget de Lisle composed 'La Marseillaise' (better known now as the French national anthem) in Strasbourg.

As a result of the industrial boom in the 19th century, the city increased its population threefold, and many of its inhabitants found themselves fleeing to the south of France to escape German occupation during World War II. In 1949, the city was chosen as the seat of the Council of Europe. Today's Strasbourg is home to the European Court of Human Rights and the European Parliament, and it plays a pivotal role in EU and international affairs. Its ambition in this area was made clear in the autumn of 2008 by the city's mayor, Roland Ries, who launched a bold – some would even say cheeky – campaign to locate all of the EU's main bodies in Strasbourg.

● *The French flag flies over the Place de la République war memorial*

Lifestyle

Strasbourg's friendly and easy-going locals appreciate the finer things in life, as the city's glut of gourmet restaurants, chichi boutiques and concert halls confirms. It won't be long before you slip into the style of this good-life city, from savouring foie gras to sipping fine wines. Yet beneath that elegant exterior lies a city with a deeply traditional heart that's firmly attached to its rural roots, where centuries-old customs still thrive, the past is well preserved and home-grown produce is a staple on every menu.

Culturally, geographically and linguistically, Strasbourg is the point where France meets Germany – mixing French finesse with Teutonic clout that goes far beyond sauerkraut and good beer. The people from Strasbourg are Alsatian and proud of it, showing a strong sense of regional identity. While the vast majority speak Alsatian, it's worth remembering this differs

● *An Alsatian browsing German books in a French city*

BRILLIANT BRAINS

The University of Strasbourg has a long history of academic excellence and today's students follow in the footsteps of famous past residents. Author, playwright and philosopher Johann Wolfgang von Goethe studied here (1768–70) and many of his poems were inspired by Notre-Dame Cathedral. Spy his statue on Place de l'Université.

from standard German. If in doubt, *parlez français*! To really impress the locals, drop a couple of Alsatian words into the conversation – it'll go down a treat.

If you think Strasbourg is just about heritage and history, though, you're in for a big surprise. Today's city shines with innovation, with the wind of change blowing through the eye-catching European Quarter where political cogs turn and the glass-and-steel Museum of Modern Art displays cutting-edge works. By night, the huge student population keeps things lively and night owls will be pleased to find one of France's funkiest after-dark scenes, from Krutenau's hip clubs to Petite France's waterfront terraces.

The proximity of the River Rhine means the city benefits from a microclimate that brings sunny, dry summers and gives the city an almost southern feel. During the warmest months, the *Strasbourgeois* can be found outdoors: the parks fill with joggers and picnickers, the pavement cafés hum and bars burst at the seams with partygoers. Socialising, seeing and being seen are important aspects of what makes Strasbourg tick.

Culture

Art and music run through Strasbourg's veins – be it sopranos on stage in one of the grand concert halls, handicrafts on display in workshops or buskers playing smooth jazz on street corners. With more than its fair share of artists, this is a city where culture is alive and tangible.

A clutch of world-class galleries means art lovers are in their element in Strasbourg. Your first stop should be the Rohan Palace's Museum of Fine Arts, where walls are graced with works by Italian Renaissance masters like Botticelli and Raphael, plus baroque and classical paintings from the likes of Rubens and Goya. To admire engravings, lithographs and drawings by Dürer, Baur and Rembrandt, make for the nearby Cabinet des Estampes et des Dessins. As well as temporary exhibitions, the luminous Museum of Modern Art has a rich permanent collection that covers painting, photography and sculpture, where you can marvel at Monet and Kandinsky originals.

Exquisite stained glass, sculpture and medieval art draw culture vultures to the Notre-Dame Museum on Place du Château. Just opposite in the Rohan Palace, pop into the excellent Archaeological Museum to glimpse everything from Bronze Age vases to Neolithic jewellery. Under the same roof, the Museum of Decorative Arts showcases a collection of Hannong ceramics and silverware in lavish state apartments. Across the river, unravel the region's intriguing heritage and history at the Alsatian Museum, where traditional living quarters have been painstakingly reconstructed to display crafts from pottery to hand-painted furniture.

◐ *The Rohan Palace's Museum of Fine Arts, Strasbourg's cultural centrepiece*

Sopranos hit the high notes, ballet dancers pirouette and classical music concerts take the stage by storm at the National Rhine Opera. To enjoy contemporary drama and cutting-edge plays, book tickets for a performance at Strasbourg National Theatre. From musicals to mime and puppetry, the famed Théâtre du Jeune Public wows young audiences with its eclectic programme of events. The acclaimed Strasbourg Philharmonic Orchestra strikes the right chord with classical music aficionados at the **Palais de la Musique et des Congrès** (ⓐ Pl. de Bordeaux ⓣ 03 88 37 67 67 ⓦ www.strasbourgmeeting.com ⓝ Tram B: Lycée Kléber).

What do satire, mime and cabaret have in common with sauerkraut? Everything at quirky arts venue La Choucrouterie, where improvised and unconventional plays in French and Alsatian raise eyebrows. A chilled place to hang out in the centre of town is cultural café L'Artichaut, where arty types turn out for performances that feature Sunday afternoon *chanson* and jazz sessions. If you love your music loud and live, **La Laiterie** (ⓐ 13 rue du Hohwald ⓣ 03 88 23 72 37 ⓦ www.laiterie.artefact.org ⓝ Tram C: Montagne Vert) won't disappoint. This funky venue stages upcoming talent and established acts, and covers the entire musical spectrum from rock to classical, folk, blues and techno.

● *Half-timbered housing, Petite France*

Shopping

Moving from wall-to-wall boutiques to antiques and from ever-so-posh speciality stores to rambling markets brimming with fresh produce, Strasbourg keeps avid shoppers on their toes. Whether you want to flex the plastic on designer labels on Grand Ile or poke around Petite France's curiosity shops, drift into your shopping spree Strasbourg-style by taking the time to linger and enjoy lunch by the waterfront.

The city's shops are open year-round, six days a week. Shopping hours are generally 10.00–19.00 Monday to Saturday, although major shopping malls like the Place des Halles stay open until 20.00. You'll find that smaller boutiques often close for lunch (12.00–14.00). A handful of shops, cafés and bakeries open on Sundays.

High-street names like Levi's and Mango cluster around the Place Kléber, Rue des Grandes Arcades and Rue du 22 Novembre. For souvenirs, delectable sweets and stuffed toy storks, make for the Place de la Cathédrale, or pick up Alsatian crafts on pretty

BEST BUYS

Gourmet lovers take home Edouard Artzner foie gras, fine Rieslings and yummy pralines from Strasbourg's top *chocolatiers*. Cuddly storks dangle in practically every shop window, and local crafts and textiles fill the shelves at Arts et Collections d'Alsace. Deck your home with handmade 'smokers', nutcrackers and nativity figures from festive shop Un Noël en Alsace.

Place-du-Marché-aux-Poissons. Fashionistas seeking the latest designs spend on labels like Hermès and Gucci on smart Rue de la Mésange, then skip over the River Ill to pick up trendy one-offs on Rue Sainte-Madeleine. Petite France's narrow streets are the place to find unique gifts from hand-thrown pots to handmade gingerbread.

The epitome of French style, Galeries Lafayette and rival department store Printemps house everything from classic to

◯ *Strasbourg's upmarket boutiques are a window-shopper's paradise*

USEFUL SHOPPING PHRASES

What time do the shops open/close?
A quelle heure ouvrent/ferment les magasins?
Ah kehlur oovr/fehrm leh mahgazhang?

How much is this?
C'est combien?
Cey combyahng?

Can I try this on?
Puis-je essayer ceci?
Pweezh ehssayeh cerssee?

My size is...
Ma taille (clothes)/
ma pointure (shoes) est ...
*Mah tie/mah
pooahngtewr ay ...*

I'll take this one, thank you
Je prends celui-ci/celle-ci, merci
*Zher prahng serlweesi/
sehlsee, mehrsee*

cutting-edge fashion, cosmetics and fragrances. Place des Halles is the city's main mall and an enjoyable one-stop shop, sheltering 120 shops, cafés and restaurants including names like FNAC, Yves Rocher and Zara.

Foodies make a beeline for the Saturday morning Farmers' Market (07.00–13.00) to bag pungent cheeses, fresh fruit and specialities like foie gras, potted snails and Alsatian honey. If you're after bric-a-brac or quality antiques, potter around Strasbourg's atmospheric flea market on Wednesdays and Saturdays (09.00–18.00), where stalls are piled high with musty books, brass and old vinyl.

Eating & drinking

A melting pot of hearty German fare and subtle French flavours, Strasbourg has taken the best ingredients from both countries to create a unique and delicious cuisine. Think garnished sauerkraut, garlicky snails and warming casseroles washed down with Riesling. The locals love their food – proved by the fact that Alsace has more Michelin star restaurants than any other French region.

If you want to savour Alsatian flavours in a *petit bistro* with views of Notre-Dame Cathedral, the Place de la Cathédrale and Place du Marché aux Cochons de Lait beckon. Romantic Petite France comes first for alfresco dining, with canalside restaurants and traditional *winstubs* (wine taverns) clustering around the Rue des Moulins and Ponts Couverts.

For cheap, filling Tunisian and Turkish snacks, head for the lively Grand Rue. World flavours spice up the hip Krutenau district, particularly along Rue de la Krutenau, Rue de Zurich and Rue d'Austerlitz, where you can savour Greek souvlaki, fiery Thai curries, Indian madras, mussels and chips – and much more.

Every Saturday from 07.00–13.00, the market on Place-du-Marché-aux-Poissons is a great chance to buy direct from local

PRICE CATEGORIES

The price ratings given in this book indicate the approximate cost of a three-course meal for one person, excluding drinks.
£ up to €25   ££ €25–45   £££ over €45

🔺 Kougelhopf – *an irresistible Alsatian speciality*

farmers and stock up on Alsatian fare for a picnic.

Strasbourg has several places where you can picnic when the sun shines, from the banks of the River Ill to the top of the Vauban Dam for panoramic canal views. Lay your blanket by the lily pond in the peaceful Botanical Gardens or the Parc de l'Orangerie's gushing fountain.

Hearty and flavoursome sums up Alsatian cuisine. If you never imagined cabbage could be exciting, try *choucroute garnie* (sauerkraut garnished with pork and sausages). Other tasty specialities you're likely to see on the menu include *baeckeoffe* (slow-cooked meat and potato casserole), *flammekueche* (crisp Alsatian pizza topped with fromage blanc, bacon and onion) and *Coq au Riesling* (chicken cooked with Riesling wine). The sweet-toothed love *kougelhopf* (a cake stuffed with plump raisins).

Vine-strewn Alsace has a wine to accompany every meal. Dry Rieslings, refreshing Sylvaners and flowery Pinot Blancs

FOIE GRAS FINESSE

At the pinnacle of haute cuisine, foie gras is savoured and served with finesse. Alsace produces 40 per cent of France's foie gras – *foie gras d'oie* (goose foie gras) with a smooth, subtle flavour, and *foie gras de canard* (duck foie gras) which is stronger and earthier. Whether fresh or semi-cooked, the foie gras you buy should have the texture of marble and the pot must be used after opening, as oxygen changes the colour and aroma.

The French serve foie gras with a glass of hot water and a spoon to scoop it into balls like a sorbet, as well as a selection of chutneys and lightly baked bread. Taste the foie gras by taking it with your fork and letting it melt on your tongue for an explosion of flavours. Goose foie gras goes well with Pinot Gris and duck foie gras with Gewürztraminer.

USEFUL DINING PHRASES

I would like a table for ... people
Je voudrais une table pour ... personnes
Zher voodray ewn tabl poor ... pehrson

Waiter/waitress!
Monsieur/Mademoiselle,
s'il vous plaît
M'sewr/madmwahzel, sylvooplay!

May I have the bill, please?
L'addition, s'il vous plaît!
Laddyssyawng, sylvooplay!

Does it have meat in it?
Est-ce que ce plat contient
de la viande?
*Essker ser plah kontyang
der lah veeahngd?*

Where is the toilet, please?
Où sont les toilettes,
s'il vous plaît?
*Oo sawng leh twahlaitt,
sylvooplay?*

complement fish and sauerkraut, while spicy Pinot Gris wines go well with foie gras and fruity Pinot Noir brings out the flavour in Munster cheese.

If you prefer the grain to the grape, Alsace produces some excellent beers including Kronenbourg, a clean and crisp lager.

The prices in most of Strasbourg's restaurants include 15 per cent service charge, but it's worth checking before you pay. If you were pleased with the meal and service, it's standard practice to round off the bill to the nearest euro or leave a small tip of around 5 per cent on the table.

Entertainment & nightlife

With a large student population that wants to have fun, a plethora of lively bars and clubs, and late licensing that keeps revellers in high spirits till the wee hours, sleepless nights in Strasbourg are pretty much guaranteed. From the illuminated Notre-Dame Cathedral to Krutenau, there's plenty of after-dark action to be had before you bid *bonne nuit*!

Night owls will be pleased to find a pick 'n' mix of late-night offerings from romantic evening boat cruises along the River Ill and improvised jazz concerts on Grand Rue to Petite France's waterfront bars and vaulted cellars with brilliant brews. Whether you're seeking traditional or trendy, a bar to unwind or a club to shake your bootie, this city comes up with the goods.

In preparation for a night on the tiles, the leisurely locals often begin with a good meal and an after-dinner stroll along the banks of the twinkling canals. The pace picks up around midnight, with most bars finishing around 02.00 and clubs keeping their doors open until 04.00.

Strasbourg is one of France's top cities for cultural highs. You'll find a generous helping of concert halls, cinemas, theatre, opera and cutting-edge arts venues. From slapstick comedy to concertos, you're well catered for here. If you want to book tickets in advance, contact the venue direct or try the **Boutique Culture** (📍 10 pl. de la Cathédrale ☎ 03 88 23 84 65 📧 boutiqueculture@cus-strasbourg.net ⏱ 12.00–19.00 Tues–Sat), covering major festivals, gigs and performances.

In Strasbourg, there is no shortage of places in which to bond with the locals over a pint (or three) of social lubricant.

◆ Head to the Strasbourg National Theatre for a night of high drama

Spiralling out from the vibrant Place de la Cathédrale, the centre's maze of narrow streets are home to some of the hottest bars and pubs, from snug cellars where you can relax with a beer on the Rue des Frères to ultra-trendy bars drawing a cocktail-sipping bunch with whom you can lock your posing horns on Rue des Grandes Arcades and Grand Rue.

If you're in the mood for chilling out over a quiet snifter, head east to arty Krutenau to mingle with a laid-back student crowd in cosy Irish pubs or bop the night away to salsa and R 'n' B rhythms. Rue de la Krutenau, Rue des Orphelins and the Quai des Bataliers are safe bets for a good night out. Expect a mellow ambience beside the canals on Petite France's lantern-lit terraces and the city's cobbled squares which buzz with life in summer.

The pubs' closing time certainly need not spell the end of the evening for those who find themselves seized by the craving for self-expression through the medium of dance. Most of the hippest clubs are around Krutenau and the suburbs, including the too-cool-to-be-true Salamandre and huge entertainment complex **Le Chalet** (ⓐ 376 route de la Wantzenau ❶ 03 88 31 18 31 ⓦ www.strasbourg-by-night.com ❶ 22.00–04.00 Fri & Sat ⓝ Bus 30: Wattwiller-Robertsau Chasseurs), where DJs on the decks spin everything from 70s disco grooves to chart hits.

Of course, this city is not all about propping up bars and throwing some shapes on the dance floor. Strasbourg has established an international reputation for its first-rate cultural venues. Among the city's major performing arts venues are the opulent National Rhine Opera on Place Broglie and Strasbourg

ENTERTAINMENT LISTINGS

Here's where to find information about entertainment and nightlife in Strasbourg.

Strass'Night For nightlife listings, pick up this handy guide from the tourist office. Ⓦ www.otstrasbourg.fr

Strassbuch Find out what's on after dark by logging onto this website. Ⓦ www.strassbuch.com

Les Dernières Nouvelles d'Alsace This French site features up-to-date info on the city's cultural scene. Ⓦ www.dna.fr

National Theatre (TNS), where the École Supérieure d'Art Dramatique ensures a varied and excellent repertoire. For tongue-in-cheek performances and avant-garde acts, make for La Choucrouterie.

Sport & relaxation

SPECTATOR SPORTS

The football-crazy locals have been waving the flag since 1906 for **Racing Club de Strasbourg** (ⓐ 12 rue de l'Extenwoerth ⓘ 03 88 44 55 44 ⓦ www.rcstrasbourg.fr). The boys in blue and white draw crowds of up to 30,000 when they play at home in La Meinau Stadium.

PARTICIPATION SPORTS

Canoeing

If you're taking a trip to Colmar, make a detour to nearby Ribeauvillé and hire a canoe or kayak to paddle through the Grand Ried wetlands. ⓐ 4 passage Carola, Ribeauvillé ⓘ 03 89 73 84 82 ⓦ www.canoes-du-ried.com

Ice skating

Those that want to slip and slide to their heart's content should get their skates on and head for France's biggest ice rink, **L'Iceberg** (ⓐ Rue Pierre Nuss ⓘ 03 90 20 14 14 ⓦ www.patinoire-iceberg.com ⓛ 14.00–18.30, 20.30–00.00 Tues & Wed, 14.00–18.30 Thur, 14.00–18.30, 20.30–00.30 Fri & Sat, 10.00–13.00, 15.00–18.30 Sun ⓝ Tram A: Rotonde. Admission charge ⓘ Times vary during school holidays.). The Olympic size rink is open year-round.

Swimming

If you fancy taking a dip in Strasbourg, there's no need to brave the chilly waters of the River Ill. In summer, join the sun-bronzed locals on the beach at Lake Baggersee, where you can swim or practise volleyball and waterpolo. The rest of the year, make for the **Bains Municipaux** (ⓐ 10 blvd de la Victoire ⓣ 03 88 25 17 58 ⓛ 08.00–19.00 Mon, 16.30–21.00 Tues, 09.00–20.00 Wed, 08.00–21.00 Thur, 08.00–20.00 Fri, 08.00–18.00 Sat, 08.00–13.00 Sun ⓝ Tram C: Gallia. Admission charge) where you can also relax with a steamy sauna or *hammam*.

Walking & cycling

Walking and pedal power are big in Strasbourg. Not only are cycling and strolling carbon-neutral ways of discovering the city, but also you'll feel fitter and will find hidden attractions. Wander at your leisure in the Parc de l'Orangerie and Botanical Gardens. Alternatively, pack boots made for walking and hike in the Vosges mountains. Hire your own set of wheels from **Vélocation** (ⓐ La Grande Verrière, pl. de la Gare ⓣ 03 88 23 56 75 ⓦ www.velocation.net) to cycle the banks of the Bruche and Marne-Rhine canals.

● *Strasbourg is two-wheel friendly*

Accommodation

Strasbourg has rooms to suit your mood and pocket – whether you're seeking cheap digs, a leafy spot to pitch your tent or an ever-so-French boutique hotel. The good news is you won't have to blow the budget to find decent accommodation in the centre, as there's everything from 16th-century half-timbered houses to snug rooms in Petite France.

HOTELS

Le Grillon £ Light-flooded rooms with polished wood floors, modern bathrooms and free Wi-Fi make this cheery hotel near the station a top budget and net-user's choice. ⓐ 2 rue Thiergarten (Petite France) ① 03 88 32 71 88 ⓦ www.grillon.com Ⓝ Tram A: Gare Centrale

Hôtel Kléber £ At the heart of the action, this charming hotel's rooms are small but perfectly formed with colour schemes ranging from cappuccino to pistachio. Spot the cathedral's spire over a leisurely breakfast. ⓐ 29 pl. Kléber (Grand Ile) ① 03 88 32 09 53 ⓕ 03 88 32 50 41 ⓦ www.hotel-kleber.com Ⓝ Tram E: Lycée Kléber

---

PRICE CATEGORIES
Gradings used in this book indicate the approximate cost of a room for two people for one night:
£ up to €65   ££ €65–120   £££ over €120

Hôtel Michelet £ This small, intimate hotel scores points for its central location. Decorated in warm hues, the rooms are basic but snug and clean. ⓐ 48 rue du Vieux Marché aux Poissons (Grand Ile) ⓣ 03 88 32 47 38 ⓦ www.hotel-michelet.com ⓝ Tram A: Grand Rue

Hôtel Patricia £ Look out for the yellow façade of this 16th-century residence set around an attractive inner courtyard. ⓐ 1a rue du Puits (Grand Ile) ⓣ 03 88 32 14 60 ⓦ www.hotelpatricia.fr ⓝ Tram A: Grand Rue

Royal Lutetia £ There's no need to dig deep for a great hotel – this place hits the mark with its contemporary design, squeaky clean bathrooms and friendly staff. Enjoy a hearty buffet breakfast. ⓐ 2 bis rue du Général Rapp (Grand Ile) ⓣ 03 88 35 20 45 ⓦ www.royal-lutetia.fr ⓝ Tram B: République

Hôtel des Arts ££ They don't come more central than this gem of a hotel overlooking a cobbled square near the cathedral. The well-kept rooms have internet access and spotless bathrooms. ⓐ 10 pl. du Marché aux Cochons de Lait (Petite France) ⓣ 03 88 37 98 37 ⓦ www.hotel-arts.com ⓝ Tram A: Grand Rue

Hôtel Couvent du Franciscain ££ Once a Franciscan monastery, this historic hotel has nice rooms with comfy beds and satellite TV. Look out for André Wenger's fresco in the vaulted breakfast room. ⓐ 18 rue du Faubourg de Pierre (Krutenau & University District) ⓣ 03 88 32 93 93 ⓦ www.hotel-franciscain.com ⓝ Bus 10: Place de Pierre

Hôtel Gutenberg ££ Relax in an Alsatian-style room with mod cons at this cosy 18th-century hotel. Petite France's attractions are on your doorstep. ⓐ 31 rue des Serruriers (Grand Ile) ⓣ 03 88 32 17 15 ⓦ www.hotel-gutenberg.com ⓝ Tram A: Grand Rue

● *View from the terrace of the Hôtel Kléber*

Hôtel Hannong ££ Bright rooms with bay windows and wood floors provide welcome respite at this central hotel, where free Wi-Fi is a real boon. The décor is a fusion of French elegance and

◔ *Elegant façade of the Hôtel Hannong*

contemporary cool. ⓐ 15 rue du 22 Novembre (Petite France)
ⓣ 03 88 32 16 22 ⓦ www.hotel-hannong.com ⓝ Tram A: Grand Rue

Hôtel Beaucour Baumann £££ You can't miss this romantic half-timbered hotel, where perks include free internet and whirlpool bathtubs. It's the perfect weekend hideaway for love-struck couples. ⓐ 5 rue des Bouchers (Krutenau & University District) ⓣ 03 88 76 72 00 ⓦ www.hotel-beaucour.com ⓝ Tram A: Porte de l'Hôpital

HOSTELS
Ciarus £ This value-for-money youth hostel offers good single, double and dorm rooms with private shower. Facilities include a 24-hour reception, bike hire, lockers and internet access. Breakfast is included. ⓐ 7 rue Finkmatt (Grand Ile) ⓣ 03 88 15 27 88 ⓦ www.ciarus.com ⓝ Bus 10: Place de Pierre

René Cassin £ A short drive from the centre of town, this chalet-style hostel is one of the best budget deals in the area. Dorms are basic but clean and airy, and linen is provided. There's a kitchen plus a bar where you can play pool. ⓐ 9 rue de l'Auberge de Jeunesse ⓣ 03 88 30 26 46 ⓦ www.fuaj.org ⓝ Tram B & C: Montagne Verte

CAMPSITES
Camping de la Montagne Verte £ Pitch a tent at this leafy campsite ten minutes' walk from Petite France. Open Mar–Dec, the site offers bike rental, and has a playground and a TV room. ⓐ 2 rue Robert Forrer ⓣ 03 86 37 95 83 ⓦ www.camping-montagne-verte-strasbourg.com ⓝ Bus 2: Nid de Cigognes

THE BEST OF STRASBOURG

TOP 10 ATTRACTIONS

- **Cathédrale de Notre-Dame (Notre-Dame Cathedral)** Grin at the gargoyles, admire the astronomical clock and climb to the top for panoramic views (see page 60)

- **Palais Rohan (Rohan Palace)** Step inside this sublime 18th-century palace to admire Neolithic artefacts and Goya artworks (see page 67)

- **Maison Kammerzell** All carved wood and stained glass, this gingerbready house serves crispy pig trotters in its vaulted restaurant (see page 64)

- **Strasbourg by boat** Board a *bâteau-mouche* to ply Strasbourg's waterways, taking in historic Petite France and the futuristic European Quarter (see page 64)

- **Ponts Couverts (Covered Bridges)** Drink in views of Petite France's canals atop these historic bridges, strung together by four 14th-century towers (see page 80)

- **Musée d'Art Moderne et Contemporain (Museum of Modern Art)** Modern art makes its mark at this crystalline gallery housing Monet and Magritte originals (see page 82)

- **Parc de l'Orangerie** Take a stroll in this flower-strewn park where storks fly overhead and picnic beside the fountained lake (see page 94)

- **La Choucrouterie** Catch avant-garde performances and try a plate of the famous *choucroute* at this former sauerkraut factory (see page 81)

- **Barrage Vauban (Vauban Dam)** Marvel at Vauban's engineering masterpiece in Petite France, with sweeping views from the top and arty surprises underground (see page 76)

- **Cave des Hospices Civils** Sniff out the world's oldest wine and unravel the city's history in these centuries-old cellars (see page 81)

🔽 *Fine detail, Notre-Dame Cathedral*

Suggested itineraries

HALF-DAY: STRASBOURG IN A HURRY

Begin your stay with a *café au lait* on one of the terraces on vibrant Place de la Cathédrale, where you'll spy the wood-carved Maison Kammerzell and Notre-Dame Cathedral's skeletal spires and striking rose window. Nip into the Rohan Palace for fine arts and impressive architecture. Head for Arts et Collections d'Alsace to pick up quality Alsatian souvenirs. Round off with a tasty *flammekueche* in Flam's Frères.

1 DAY: TIME TO SEE A LITTLE MORE

Climb Notre-Dame Cathedral's tower for bird's-eye views, then hop aboard a *bateau-mouche* to chug along the River Ill, glimpsing Petite France's string of half-timbered houses and the crystalline European Quarter. Walk around the Covered Bridges and Vauban Dam to admire the city's lattice of canals. Grab a chair at a bistro in Petite France for a hearty Alsatian lunch. Spend the afternoon wallowing in contemporary works from Kandinsky to Picasso at the glass-fronted Museum of Modern Art. As dusk falls, stroll through Petite France's narrow alleyways, pausing to sample Trappist brews at the Académie de la Bière.

2–3 DAYS: TIME TO SEE MUCH MORE

Trace regional heritage in the Alsatian Museum or find age-old wines in the Cave des Hospices Civils. Those keen to see Strasbourg's lesser-known side make for the Krutenau and University districts for a boho vibe and breath of fresh air. Rest beside the lily pond in the Botanical Gardens or amble down Parc de l'Orangerie's chestnut tree-lined avenues (keep your eye open for storks). If you're feeling active, hire a bike to pedal along the Marne-Rhine canal. After dark, La Choucrouterie serves Alsatian sauerkraut with sausages and hosts improvised performances. The National Rhine Opera reels in classical music buffs.

LONGER: ENJOYING STRASBOURG TO THE FULL

Linger to appreciate all Strasbourg has to offer before exploring Alsace's hidden gems. At the foot of the Vosges mountains, Saverne is home to medieval Greifenstein Castle, a Franciscan monastery and magnificent rose gardens. Stepping south, Colmar is picture-perfect Alsace. Discover Little Venice's beautiful canals, shop for foie gras and taste home-grown wines straight from the barrel. Culture vultures make for the Bartholdi Museum, birthplace of the Statue of Liberty's creator, and Unterlinden Museum housed in a Dominican convent.

● *Boarding a* bâteau-mouche *is one of the best ways to see the city*

Something for nothing

The best things in Strasbourg are free. If you want cultural highs, come on the first Sunday of the month when all museums are free, including the Alsatian Museum, Museum of Modern Art and Rohan Palace. For open-air entertainment, look no further than Place de la Cathédrale where musicians, jugglers, mime artists and puppeteers frequently perform in the shadow of Notre-Dame. There's no better place to get a cultural fix than the arty L'Artichaut on Grand Rue, which regularly hosts live jazz and jam sessions for free or next to nothing.

One of the city's greatest and cheapest pleasures is soaking up its vibrant street life. Kick off your stay with a walk along the banks of the River Ill to Petite France to gaze up at charming half-timbered houses with wonky rooflines and inner courtyards, once home to the city's tanners, millers and fishermen. This picturesque district is home to a clutch of attractions which you can enjoy for free – from the Vauban Dam affording sweeping city views to Gothic St Thomas' Church (step inside to see the Silbermann organ).

Need a breath of fresh air? Strasbourg has plenty of parks and gardens tucked up its green sleeve, where you can have a leisurely stroll or relax with a picnic. Begin in the Botanical Gardens fringed with Alsatian vines and fragrant pines, then take a hike past chestnut trees, fountains and brightly coloured flowers in the Parc de l'Orangerie. The Parc de la Citadelle is a superb chance to trace the past with an amble along the city's fortifications, the striking remains of Vauban's citadel.

Every year, Strasbourg draws crowds to its calendar of free

festivals and events. The *Journées du Patrimoine* (Heritage Days) are a highlight in September when all of the city's key cultural venues and institutions fling open their doors to the public. The *Nuit des Musées* (Night of Museums) reels in culture buffs with free after-dark activities and entry to all museums and galleries. In summer, the **Fête de la Musique** (Ⓦ www.strasbourg.info/events) brings a host of free concerts to the city.

🔺 *The Parc de l'Orangerie, one of Strasbourg's many green spaces*

When it rains

With plenty of indoor attractions to discover, there's no need to let sudden showers put a dampener on your stay in Strasbourg. If it's nippy outside, warm up in one of the city's cosy *winstubs* or wood-panelled bistros. The atmospheric L'Ancienne Douane and medieval cellar Caveau Gurtlerhoft dish up flavoursome Alsatian fare in a snug setting that will help you to forget the wet weather.

When the skies open, take shelter in one of the city's superb galleries or museums. You can spend an entire day exploring the sumptuous ceramics, fine arts and prehistoric artefacts on display at the Rohan Palace. Brush up against famous works by Picasso, Kandinsky and Magritte in the Museum of Modern Art, before enjoying lunch in the ultramodern Art Café. Below the ground, the weather never changes, making the cellar vaults of Cave des Hospices Civils a top rainy-day choice – take a tour and be sure to spot (not sample!) the world's oldest wine dating back to 1472.

There's nothing like a shopping spree to make everything seem brighter, and Strasbourg has got this covered. Pick of the bunch is the sprawling Place des Halles mall, where you'll find 120 shops huddling under one roof including names like Zara, Morgan and Sephora, as well as a cinema, cafés and restaurants. In the centre, French department stores like Galeries Lafayette and Printemps beckon fashion divas wanting to escape the drizzle.

Adopt the locals' love of leisurely coffee drinking and watching *le monde* go by. Grand Ile and Petite France have more than their fair share of inviting cafés, where you can sink into a sofa to read the newspapers, chat and philosophise over a steaming mug of coffee. The Alsatians have a sweet tooth, and their delicious cakes and pastries are the ultimate drab day pick-me-up, especially the famous *kougelhopf*. Alternatively, pull up a chair at one of Strasbourg's old-world taverns like the Académie de la Bière and Frères Berthom for fine brews and a homely feel.

⬤ *There's nowhere better to spend a rainy hour than a* pâtisserie

On arrival

TIME DIFFERENCE

Strasbourg runs on Central European Time (CET), an hour ahead of Greenwich Mean Time. During Daylight Saving Time (mid-March to mid-October) clocks are put forward one hour.

ARRIVING

By air

Situated 10 km (6 miles) from the city centre, **Strasbourg-Entzheim International Airport** (ⓐ Entzheim ⓣ 03 88 64 67 67 ⓦ www.strasbourg.aeroport.fr) is served by ten airlines including Air France, Olympic Airlines and Iberia. These operate a frequent and direct service to, e.g., Amsterdam, Brussels, Istanbul, Madrid, Paris and London Gatwick. You'll find good duty-free shopping, bars and restaurants in the main terminal building.

The airport is a 15-minute drive from central Strasbourg on the A35 motorway. Shuttle buses linking the airport to Baggersee tram station depart every 20 minutes at peak and every 40 minutes at off-peak hours daily. Taxis are available from the rank in front of the terminal.

Alternatively, fly to **Baden Airpark** (ⓐ Victoria Boulevard 124, Rheinmünster ⓣ 07229 66 2000 ⓦ www.badenairpark.de) in Germany (a 35-minute drive from Strasbourg), home to no-frills airline Ryanair and Air Berlin. Car hire, taxis and shuttle bus connections are available.

By rail

Strasbourg's **main station** (ⓐ Pl. de la Gare ⓣ 08 92 35 35 35 www.sncf.fr) on Place de la Gare is a five-minute walk from the centre. SNCF and TER trains operate an efficient rail service to key French cities such as Paris, Bordeaux, Lyon and Lille, as well as European destinations such as Brussels, Munich, Vienna, Stuttgart and Rome. The introduction of high-speed TGV trains has cut journey times considerably. There are shops, toilets and left luggage lockers at the station.

By road

The city's central bus station (*gare routière*) is located on Place des Halles. The **Strasbourg Transportation Company** (CTS, Pl. des Halles 03 88 77 70 70 www.cts-strasbourg.fr) runs buses to the suburbs and nearby villages. Operating a Europe-wide service, Eurolines pull up in front of the Citroën garage on Rue Maréchal Lefevre.

 Tramlines criss-cross the city

Close to the Franco-German border, Strasbourg is easy to access by car. The A4, A32, A34 and A352 motorways link the city to nearby places such as Baden-Baden, Paris, Amsterdam and Brussels.

Driving tends to be quite relaxed in Strasbourg, particularly if you plan your journey outside of rush hour (🕐 08.00–09.30, 16.30–18.30 Mon–Fri). Parking is generally affordable and one of the cheapest central options is Halles. Expect to pay around €9 for 24-hour parking.

FINDING YOUR FEET

Strasbourg is like a charming Alsatian village that has outgrown its small-town boots. Mixing the German love of logic with the French *joie de vivre*, the city is easy to negotiate and has a laid-back vibe thanks to the large number of students living there.

The friendly, bilingual locals are welcoming to travellers. Most speak some English and are more than happy to help you find your way.

❶ Strasbourg is generally a safe city and the crime rate is low. However, pickpocketing can be a problem in touristy areas such as Place de la Cathédrale, Grand Rue and the River Ill.

ORIENTATION

Situated in Alsace's northeastern corner, just a few miles from the German border, the French city of Strasbourg is fringed to the east by the snaking River Rhine.

Encircled by the River Ill, the Grand Ile is the epicentre of Strasbourg, where all roads lead to the cobbled Place de la Cathédrale dominated by the immense bulk of Notre-Dame

IF YOU GET LOST, TRY …

Do you speak English?
Parlez-vous anglais?
Pahrlayvoo ahnglay?

Is this the way to…?
C'est la bonne direction pour…?
Seh lah bon deerekseeawng poor…?

Can you point to it on my map?
Pouvez-vous me le montrer sur la carte?
Poovehvoo mer ler mawngtreh sewr lah kart?

Cathedral. Edging west of the centre is Petite France, interlaced with canals. Go east to reach buzzing Krutenau and the University District.

GETTING AROUND
On foot
In a city so compact, where most attractions are in or around the centre, walking is not only the best but often the only way to get around. The tourist office provides free maps.

By bike
With more than 350 km (217 miles) of marked cycling trails, Strasbourg is made for cycling. If you fancy hiring your own set of wheels to discover the city and surrounding region your first stop should be Vélocation (see page 36), renting quality bikes at competitive rates.

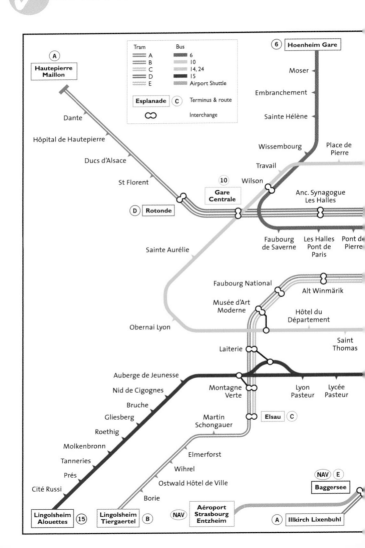

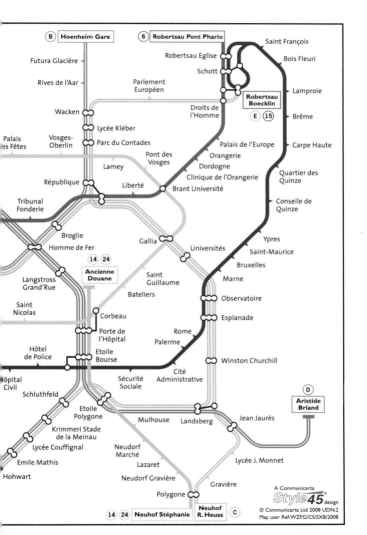

By tram

Five tram lines (A, B, C, D and E) operate daily 04.30–00.30. The modern trams are an efficient and scenic way to get around. You can purchase your tickets at the automatic ticket machines at each stop.

By bus

Strasbourg's buses may not be the fastest means of travel, but the city's 23 lines cover most areas and its suburbs 04.30–23.30. The CTS 24-hour pass allowing unlimited use of the tram and bus network is excellent value.

CAR HIRE

While the city's public transport network is great for getting about town, it's a good idea to hire a car if you're planning on exploring more rural areas of Alsace.

Budget ⓐ 14 rue Déserte ⓣ 03 88 52 87 52 ⓦ www.budget.com ⓛ 08.00–12.00, 14.00–18.00 Mon–Fri, 08.00–12.00 Sat

Sixt ⓐ Blvd de Nancy ⓣ 03 88 23 72 72 ⓦ www.e-sixt.com ⓛ 08.00–12.00, 14.00–18.00 Mon–Fri, 08.00–12.00 Sat

ⓞ *Giant clock face, Notre-Dame Cathedral*

Grand Ile

Imagine a rabbit's warren of narrow cobbled streets, gabled houses the colour of candy and tree-fringed squares sprouting world-class museums and you're getting close to Grand Ile, a UNESCO World Heritage Site. Dominated by the immense Notre-Dame Cathedral and humming with life in pavement cafés, central Strasbourg is the stuff of fairytales.

SIGHTS & ATTRACTIONS

Cathédrale de Notre-Dame (Notre-Dame Cathedral)

A riot of skinny spires, flying buttresses and gargoyles, Strasbourg's Gothic giant rises like a vision. The interior impresses with its cross-ribbed vaulting, huge rose window and astronomical clock. For views over the city's pointy rooftops, climb 332 steps to the top of the tower. ⓐ Pl. de la Cathédrale ❶ 03 88 21 43 34 ⓦ www.cathedrale-strasbourg.asso.fr ❶ 07.00–11.20, 12.35–19.00 ⓝ Tram A: Grand Rue. Admission charge

> ### SOARING SPIRES
> Strasbourg's beautiful cathedral rose to fame as the world's tallest building from 1439 to 1847 and held the title of highest church until 1880 when it was upstaged by Cologne's *Dom*. For centuries, the enormous structure has inspired philosophers, artists and writers including Victor Hugo who described it as 'a veritable tiara of stone'.

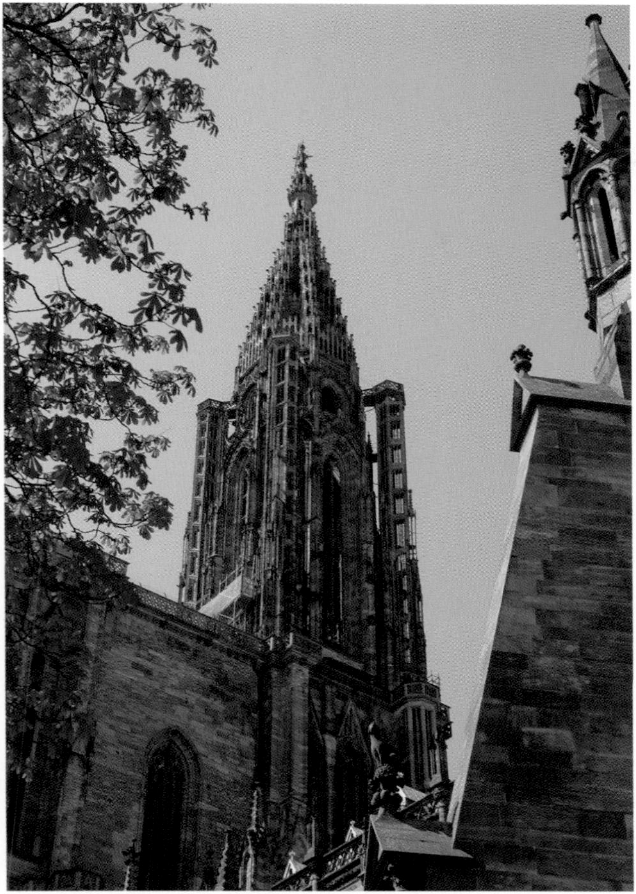

The towering Gothic spire of Notre-Dame Cathedral

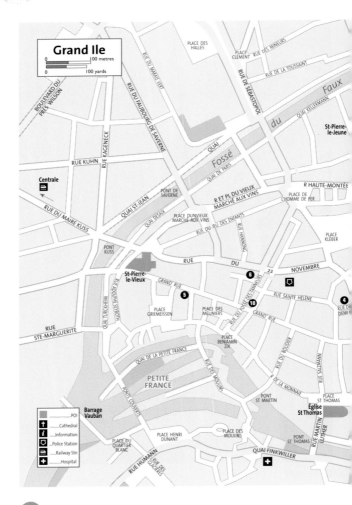

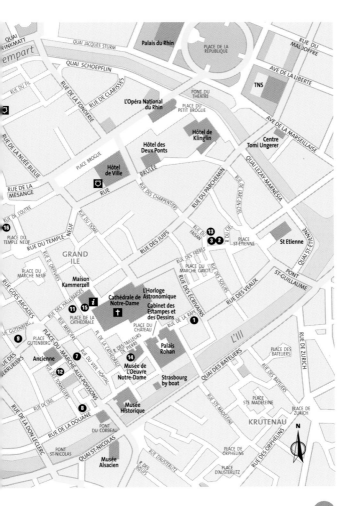

QUAI FINKMATT

QUAI JACQUES STURM

QUAI SCHOEPFLIN

empart

QUAI DU MALJOFFRE

RUE DU MALJOFFRE

Palais du Rhin

PLACE DE LA RÉPUBLIQUE

AVE DE LA LIBERTE

TNS

RUE DU FIL

RUE DE LA FONDERIE

RUE DE CLARISSES

L'Opéra National du Rhin

PONT DU THÉÂTRE

PLACE DU PETIT BROGLIE

AVE DE LA MARSEILLAISE

Hôtel de Klinglin

Centre Tomi Ungerer

RUE DE LA NUÉE BLEUE

PLACE BROGLIE

Hôtel des Deux Ponts

QUAI LEZAY-MARNESIA

RUE DE LA MÉSANGE

Hôtel de Ville

BRÛLÉE

RUE

RUE DES CHARPENTIERS

RUE DU PARCHEMIN

RUE DU PRE-EN-CIEL

RUE DE L'OUTRE

RUE DU TEMPLE-NEUF

RUE DU DÔME

RUE DES JUIFS

RUE DU FAISAN

RUE DE LA CIGOGNE

PLACE ST-ETIENNE

St Etienne

QUAI ST-ETIENNE

16

PLACE DU TEMPLE NEUF

GRAND ILE

PLACE DU MARCHE NEUF

RUE DES ORFÈVRES

Maison Kammerzell

RUE DES FRÈRES

PLACE DU MARCHE GAYOT

RUE DES SOEURS

RUE DES ÉCRIVAINS

PONT ST-GUILLAUME

13

3 2

RUE DES GDES ARCADES

RUE GUTENBERG

9

PLACE GUTENBERG

RUE DES HALLEBARDES

i

11 15

Cathédrale de Notre-Dame

PLACE DE LA CATHÉDRALE

RUE MERCIÈRE

RUE DU VIEL HÔPITAL

L'Horloge Astronomique

Cabinet des Estampes et des Dessins

PLACE DU CHÂTEAU

R. DES TAILLEURS DE PIERRE

1

RUE DE LA RAPE

RUE DES VEAUX

L'ILL

PLACE DES BATELIERS

RUE DE ZURICH

PLACE DES SERRURIERS

Ancienne

7

12

RUE DE LA DOUANE

8

RUE DU MARCHE-AUX-POISSONS

14

Musée de L'Oeuvre Notre-Dame

Palais Rohan

Strasbourg by boat

QUAI DES BATELIERS

RUE DES BATELIERS

RUE DE L'OUTIL

RUE DU NOYER

Musée Historique

PONT DU CORBEAU

PLACE STE MADELEINE

PLACE DE ZURICH

RUE ST-MARGUERITE

KRUTENAU

N

RUE DE LA DON LECLERC

PONT ST-NICOLAS

QUAI ST-NICOLAS

Musée Alsacien

R. DES VEAUX

RUE D'AUSTERLITZ

PLACE DE ORPHELINS

RUE DES ORPHELINS

PLACE D'AUSTERLITZ

L'Horloge Astronomique (Astronomical Clock)

Showing the movement of the earth, sun and moon, the cathedral's astronomical clock is a mechanical marvel. The 12 apostles file past Christ as a cock crows thrice and cherubs turn hourglasses. ⓐ Pl. de la Cathédrale ⓑ Parade of the Apostles: 12.30 ⓝ Tram A: Grand Rue. Admission charge

Maison Kammerzell

This gingerbready house built in 1427 is one of the city's most iconic landmarks. ⓐ 16 pl. de la Cathédrale ⓣ 03 88 32 42 14 ⓦ www.maison-kammerzell.com ⓝ Tram A: Grand Rue.

Strasbourg by boat

A great way to spot Strasbourg's key sights is to hop aboard one of the *bâteau-mouche* boats plying the River Ill. Hour-long tours take in highlights including Petite France's half-timbered houses and the crystalline European Quarter. ⓐ Palais Rohan Port ⓣ 03 88 32 75 25 ⓦ www.strasbourg.port.fr ⓛ 10.00, 14.30, 16.00 Jan–Mar; 09.30–21.00 Apr & Oct; 09.30–22.00 May–Sept ⓝ Tram A: Grand Rue. Admission charge

CULTURE

Cabinet des Estampes et des Dessins

Art buffs can admire 200,000 works spanning five centuries at this superb museum. Moving from fine arts to architecture and history, the collection of engravings, lithographs, carvings and paintings features pieces by Finiguerra, Goya, Rembrandt and Mantegna. ⓐ 5 pl. du Château ⓣ 03 88 52 50 00 ⓛ 12.00–18.00

◐ *The carved wooden façade of the Maison Kammerzell*

Mon, Wed–Fri, 10.00–18.00 Sat & Sun Tram A: Grand Rue. Admission charge

Centre Tomi Ungerer

Unearth one-offs by Strasbourg-born artist Tomi Ungerer at this museum displaying his illustrations, posters and intriguing toy collection. ⓐ 2 av. de la Marseillaise ❶ 03 69 06 37 27 ⓛ 12.00–18.00 Mon, Wed–Fri, 10.00–18.00 Sat & Sun ⓝ Tram B: République. Admission charge

Musée Alsacien (Alsatian Museum)

Trace Alsace's rural heritage at this doll's house-like museum by the river, where displays cover farming, crafts and customs from the 8th to the 19th centuries. The living quarters have been meticulously reconstructed and highlights include the wood-panelled Alcôve de la Stube. ⓐ 23–25 quai Saint-Nicolas ❶ 03 88 52 50 01 ⓛ 12.00–18.00 Mon, Wed–Fri, 10.00–18.00 Sat & Sun ⓝ Tram A: Porte de l'Hôpital. Admission charge

Musée de l'Oeuvre Notre-Dame (Notre-Dame Museum)

Housing one of Europe's top collections of medieval art, this museum showcases a peerless collection of stained-glass windows, sculpture, intricate wood carvings and religious art. Be sure to glimpse the pretty Gothic garden. ⓐ 3 pl. du Château ❶ 03 88 52 50 00 ⓛ 12.00–18.00 Mon, Wed–Fri, 10.00–18.00 Sat & Sun ⓝ Tram A: Grand Rue. Admission charge

L'Opéra National du Rhin (National Rhine Opera)

Towering above the tree-fringed Place Broglie, Strasbourg's

columned opera house reels in culture vultures with first-rate classical concerts, opera and dance. ⓐ 19 pl. Broglie
ⓣ 03 88 75 48 00 ⓦ www.opera-national-du-rhin.com
ⓛ Season Oct–July ⓝ Tram B: Broglie

Palais Rohan (Rohan Palace)

The spitting image of Versailles (albeit on a smaller scale), this grand 18th-century edifice is the former palace of prince-bishops and shelters a trio of museums. Behind the blushing bricks you'll discover artefacts from mammoth bones to Neolithic vases in the Archaeological Museum. On the ground floor, the Museum of Decorative Arts features sublime state apartments plus a collection of Hannong ceramics and clocks. The first floor is given over to the Museum of Fine Arts with a clutch of Rubens, Goya and El Greco masterpieces. ⓐ 2 pl. du Château
ⓣ 03 88 52 50 00 ⓦ www.musees-strasbourg.org ⓛ 10.00–18.00
Wed–Mon. Admission charge

TNS (Strasbourg National Theatre)

The resident École Supérieure d'Art Dramatique ensures a rich and varied repertoire at this monumental theatre rising above Place de la République. Cutting-edge plays headline the programme. ⓐ Pl. de la République ⓣ 03 88 24 88 00
ⓦ www.tns.fr ⓛ Season Sept–May ⓝ Tram B: République

RETAIL THERAPY

Arganya If you can't get to the souks of Marrakech, this mosaic-tiled speciality store is the next best thing. Browse the terrific selection of Moroccan sweets, teas, crafts and cosmetics in authentic surroundings. 13 rue des Veaux 03 88 36 73 91 10.00–19.30 Mon, 08.00–19.30 Tues & Wed, 08.00–21.00 Thur–Sat, 11.00–19.00 Sun Tram C: République

Arts et Collections d'Alsace Pick up quality regional crafts from stained glass to embroidered tablecloths made using traditional methods in this rustic store near the river. 4 pl.-du-Marché-aux-Poissons 03 88 14 03 77 www.artsetco.perso.cegetel.net 14.00–19.00 Mon, 10.00–19.00 Tues–Fri, 09.00–19.00 Sat Tram A: Grand Rue

La Chapellerie Those with a head for hats can purchase quirky kopf creations at this boutique. 27 pl. de la Cathédrale 03 88 21 93 00 14.00–19.00 Mon, 10.00–19.00 Tues–Fri, 10.00–18.30 Sat Tram A: Grand Rue

La Cloche à Fromage Sniff out 200 types of cheese at this *fromage*-crazy delicatessen. You can sample them in the adjoining restaurant. 32 rue des Tonneliers 03 88 52 04 03 14.00–18.00 Mon, 10.15–12.15, 13.30–19.00 Tues, Thur & Fri, 10.30–12.30, 14.30–19.30 Wed, 10.15–19.00 Sat Tram A: Grand Rue

La Cure Gourmande The scent of butter fills the air at this shop lined with racks of biscuits, bonbons and stripy lollipops. The chocolate olives are divine. 5 rue Mercière 03 88 32 97 49 08.30–19.30 Tram A: Grand Rue

🔺 *Treasure or trash? Decide for yourself at the Flea Market*

Edouard Artzner Look out for the white geese at the entrance to this temple of fine foie gras. **ⓐ** 7 rue de la Mésange **ⓣ** 03 88 32 05 00 **ⓦ** www.edouard-artzner.com **ⓛ** 15.00–19.00 Mon, 09.00–19.00 Tues–Fri, 08.30–18.30 Sat **ⓝ** Tram B: Broglie

Farmers' Market Stalls are piled high with round cheeses, shiny fruits and fresh fish at this buzzy farmers' market. Fill your bags with locally produced honey, foie gras, potted snails and ripe camembert for a picnic by the Ill. **ⓐ** Pl.-du-Marché-aux-Poissons **ⓛ** 07.00–13.00 Sat **ⓝ** Tram A: Grand Rue

Flea Market Antique lovers poke around this street market crammed with musty books, brass, old records and Belle Époque furniture. It's a nice place to potter even if you don't want to buy anything. **ⓐ** Rue du Vieil-Hôpital **ⓛ** 09.00–18.00 Wed & Sat **ⓝ** Tram A: Grand Rue

Galeries Lafayette This sprawling department store stocks everything from fashion to fragrances. **ⓐ** 34 rue du 22 Novembre **ⓣ** 03 88 15 23 00 **ⓛ** 09.00–19.30 Mon–Sat **ⓝ** Tram A: Homme de Fer

Place des Halles The ideal one-stop shop, 120 high-street stores including Mango, Zara, Agatha and Sephora cluster in this modern mall. Food options are also available. **ⓐ** 24 pl. des Halles **ⓣ** 03 88 22 21 61 **ⓦ** www.placedeshalles.com **ⓛ** 09.00–20.00 Mon–Sat **ⓝ** Tram A: Ancienne Synagogue les Halles

TAKING A BREAK

Bistrot & Chocolat £ ❶ With a boho feel and young, friendly staff, this is one of Strasbourg's most laid-back spots. Tucked behind the cathedral, the café is famous for its waffles and delectable pralines, but you can also refuel on soups, samosas and vegetarian dishes prepared with organic ingredients. ⓐ 8 rue de la Râpe ⓣ 03 88 36 39 60 ⓛ 09.00–19.00 Tues–Fri, 09.00–19.30 Sat, 10.00–19.00 Sun ⓝ Tram A: Grand Rue

Crep' Mili £ ❷ Sugary, savoury and simply moreish, this 17th-century cellar whips up 60 different varieties of Breton crêpes. ⓐ 3 rue du Ciel ⓣ 03 88 36 56 88 ⓛ 11.30–14.00, 18.30–23.30 Mon–Sat, 18.30–11.30 Sun ⓝ Tram B: Broglie

Flam's Frères £ ❸ This buzzing restaurant's crowning glory is its light, crisp *flammekueche*. The prices won't break the bank either. ⓐ 29 rue des Frères ⓣ 03 88 36 36 90 ⓦ www.flams.fr ⓛ 12.00–23.00 ⓝ Tram B: Broglie

Mooze £ ❹ This bright and airy Japanese restaurant prides itself on excellent sushi. See your lunch drift past on the moving platform. ⓐ 1 rue de la Demi-Lune ⓣ 03 88 22 68 46 ⓛ 12.00–15.30, 19.00–00.30 Mon–Sat ⓝ Tram A: Grand Rue

La Part Thé £ ❺ Refuel with salads, pastries and ice cream in this light-flooded café on one of Strasbourg's main drags. ⓐ 42 Grand Rue ⓣ 03 88 32 20 83 ⓛ 07.30–19.00 Mon–Fri, 07.30–18.00 Sat, 08.30–18.00 Sun ⓝ Tram A: Grand Rue

La Petite Pause £ ❻ Create your own sandwich at this café serving yummy baguettes and salads. ⓐ 47B rue du Fossé-des-Tanneurs ⓣ 03 88 22 51 17 ⓛ 10.30–15.00 Mon–Sat ⓝ Tram A: Grand Rue

Le Roi et son Fou £ ❼ Perfect for people-watching, this classic French bistro is the place to relax with a *café au lait* or light lunch on the pavement terrace. ⓐ 37 rue du Vieil-Hôpital ⓣ 03 88 23 22 22 ⓛ 08.00–20.00 Mon–Sat, 09.00–20.00 Sun ⓝ Tram A: Grand Rue

AFTER DARK

RESTAURANTS

L'Ancienne Douane £ ❽ Dating back to 1358, this moody brasserie by the water's edge serves hearty Alsatian fare and a slice of history. Wood panelling and warm colours create an inviting atmosphere to enjoy tasty onion tart with lashings of sauerkraut. ⓐ 6 rue de la Douane ⓣ 03 88 15 78 78 ⓦ www.anciennedouane.fr ⓛ 12.00–14.00, 19.00–22.00 ⓝ Tram A: Grand Rue

Aux Armes de Strasbourg £ ❾ This quintessential French brasserie with a terrace on the square scores points for its warm ambience and local specialities – try the Alsatian snails or sausage salad. ⓐ 9 pl. Gutenberg ⓣ 03 88 32 85 62 ⓛ 11.30–00.00 ⓝ Tram A: Homme de Fer

La Case de l'Isle Bourbon £ ❿ For an authentic taste of the Indian Ocean, pull up a chair at this little gem of a restaurant dishing up spicy Réunion pork curry and lychee punch.

ⓐ 34 Grand Rue ⓣ 03 88 32 60 93 ⓛ 12.00–14.00, 18.30–00.00 Tues–Sat, 12.00–14.00 Sun & Mon ⓝ Tram A: Grand Rue

Caveau Gurtlerhoft £ ⑪ Steps wind down to this wood-beamed cellar, where canons stored their wine in the Middle Ages. The menu features favourites like rösti potatoes and fish sauerkraut. ⓐ 13 pl. de la Cathédrale ⓣ 03 88 75 00 75 ⓦ www.gurtlerhoft.com ⓛ 11.45–13.45, 18.45–21.45 ⓝ Tram A: Grand Rue

Au Petit Tonnelier £ ⑫ The décor at this smart restaurant sums up minimalist chic. Savour classics with a contemporary twist like asparagus gratin and calamari penne. ⓐ 16 rue des Tonneliers ⓣ 03 88 32 53 54 ⓦ www.aupetittonnelier.com ⓛ 12.00–14.00, 19.00–22.30 Sun–Fri, 12.00–14.00, 19.00–23.00 Sat ⓝ Tram A: Grand Rue

Tiger Wok £ ⑬ Smoked tofu and crunchy lotus stalks fresh from the wok are the appeal of this trendy Thai noodle bar. Choose your ingredients and let the *wokeur* work his high-flamed magic. ⓐ 8 rue du Faisan ⓣ 03 88 36 44 87 ⓦ www.tigerwok.com ⓛ 12.00–14.15, 19.00–22.30 Sun–Tues, 12.00–14.15, 19.00–23.00 Wed & Thur, 12.00–14.15, 19.00–23.30 Fri & Sat ⓝ Tram A: Homme de Fer

Le Tire Bouchon £ ⑭ With its huge barrels, creeping vines and cavernous wine cellar, it's little wonder this charming *winstub* is called 'the corkscrew'. Expect well-prepared Alsatian fare like *lewerknepfle* (liver dumplings) and sander fillet in Riesling sauce. ⓐ 5 rue des Tailleurs de Pierre ⓣ 03 88 22 16 32

Ⓦ www.letirebouchon.fr Ⓛ 12.00–14.30, 18.30–00.00
Ⓝ Tram B: Broglie

Maison Kammerzell ££ Ⓑ A favourite gastro haunt, this
picture-perfect restaurant opposite the cathedral has
a medieval feel. Stained-glass windows, vaulted ceilings
and pastoral frescoes set the scene for flavoursome dishes
like *baeckoffe* stew, coq au Riesling and crispy pig trotters.
Ⓐ 16 pl. de la Cathédrale Ⓣ 03 88 32 42 14 Ⓦ www.maison-
kammerzell.com Ⓝ Tram A: Grand Rue

Au Crocodil £££ Ⓑ Foodies splash out on Michelin-starred cuisine
at this sky-lit restaurant, where innovative chef Emile Jung cooks
up a storm using the freshest Alsatian produce. Creative flavours
include quail stuffed with goose liver, figs and walnuts. Fixed price
menus offer the best value and booking is essential. Ⓐ 10 rue de
l'Outre Ⓣ 03 88 32 13 02 Ⓦ www.au-crocodile.com Ⓛ 12.00–13.30,
19.30–21.30 Tues–Sat Ⓝ Tram B: Broglie

BARS & CLUBS
L'Artichaut The arty 'artichoke' has its finger on the pulse of the
centre's cultural scene. This funky café decked out with modern
art has live jazz, games and literary events. Ⓐ 56 Grand Rue
Ⓣ 03 88 22 13 26 Ⓦ www.lartichaut.fr Ⓛ 11.30–01.00 Tues–Sat,
13.00–21.00 Sun Ⓝ Tram A: Grand Rue

Les Aviateurs Hollywood stars grace the walls of this 1950s bar
in the centre. A real blast from the past, this popular enclave
serves cool drinks and big screen sports. Ⓐ 12 rue des Soeurs

03 88 36 52 69 www.les-aviateurs.com 20.30–04.00
Tram A: Porte de l'Hôpital

Bar Exils You can't beat a lively pub with beer on tap, darts, squishy sofas and a laid-back feel. That's exactly what you'll get here.
28 rue de l'Ail 03 88 32 52 70 www.barexils.com 12.00–04.00 Mon–Fri, 14.00–04.00 Sat & Sun Tram A: Grand Rue

Au Brasseur Put your beer goggles on and head to this micro-brewery serving great beer and *flammekueche* in the cosy cellar.
22 rue des Veaux 03 88 36 12 13 11.30–01.00 Mon–Sat, 11.30–00.00 Sun Tram B: Broglie

Les Frères Berthom Amber nectar lovers head for this self-proclaimed 'beer village'. The cave-like bar complete with cobblestones, snug nooks and gnarled trees serves some of the city's finest Trappist brews. 18 rue des Tonneliers 03 88 32 81 18 www.lesfreresberthom.com 15.00–01.00 Mon & Tues, 15.00–01.30 Wed & Thur, 12.00–02.30 Fri & Sat Tram A: Grand Rue

Jeanette et les Cycleux Born to be wild, Jeanette promises 'no sex, no drugs, but rock 'n' roll'. Chrome motorbikes hang from the walls in this retro-style bar playing 1960s and 70s grooves. 30 rue des Tonneliers 03 88 23 02 71 11.00–01.30 Tram A: Grand Rue

Schlosserstub Low beams and smooth jazz add to the easy vibe here. Chill with a beer and check out the board games.
25 rue des Serruriers 03 88 32 02 60 08.00–01.00 Mon–Sat, 15.00–21.00 Sun Tram A: Grand Rue

Petite France

Criss-crossed with canals and punctuated with pastel-hued half-timbered houses where millers, tanners and fishermen once lived, Petite France looks as though it has stepped straight out of a Grimm's fairytale. From the giddy heights of the Vauban Dam to the depths of the Cave des Hospices Civils, this waterfront district oozes history from every pore. Awash with geraniums, arched with bridges and laced with twisty cobbled streets, this is Alsace at its picture-book best – pristine, well preserved and sitting pretty.

SIGHTS & ATTRACTIONS

Barrage Vauban (Vauban Dam)

At the top of every must-see list is Strasbourg's eye-catching dam, the brainchild of military engineer Sébastien le Prestre de Vauban who designed it in 1690 to protect the city from a river attack. The dam's inside is like a giant honeycomb, riddled with tunnels and chambers. But it's the viewing platform that takes your breath away. Perched high above Petite France, the terrace affords far-reaching views of the covered bridges and the city's lattice of canals. Walk through the main passage to glimpse stone statues and contemporary art installations behind wrought iron gates, which build up to the Museum of Modern Art on the other side. ⓐ Pl. Hans Jean Arp ⓛ Tunnel: 07.30–19.30; terrace: 09.00–19.30 ⓝ Tram B: Altwinmärik

Église St Thomas (St Thomas' Church)

Among the city's best-kept secrets, this rose-hued Gothic church with its wistful tower and turrets sits on Romanesque foundations and shelters the golden Silbermann organ on which Mozart played in 1778. Step inside to spy Marshal Maurice of Saxony's tomb and Albert Schweitzer's organ. ⓐ 11 rue Martin Luther ⓣ 03 88 32 14 46 ⓛ 14.00–17.00 Jan & Feb; 10.00–17.00 Mar, Nov & Dec; 10.00–18.00 Apr–Oct ⓝ Tram A: Grand Rue

● *The Vauban Dam affords spectacular views over Petite France*

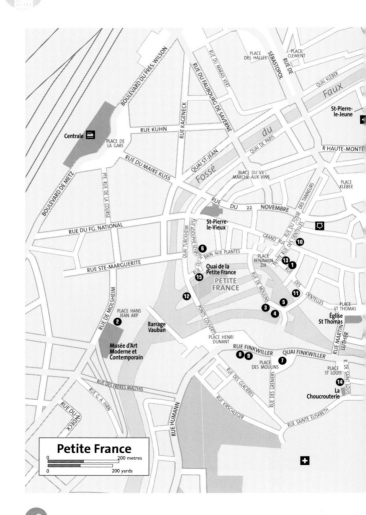

Petite France

0 _____ 200 metres

0 _____ 200 yards

Ponts Couverts (Covered Bridges)

Four striking stone towers link together the covered bridges, the remains of the city's sturdy ramparts and one of Strasbourg's most iconic landmarks. The wood-and-tile roof that covered the bridges was actually removed in the 18th century, but they have kept the name to this day. Smothered in brightly coloured flowers, the curvaceous bridges offer prime views of the boats that chug up the River Ill and the Vauban Dam. ⓐ Rue des Ponts Couverts ⓝ Tram B: Altwinmärik

🔺 *Four massive towers link the Covered Bridges (Ponts Couverts) together*

Quai de la Petite France

Fringed with chestnut, plane and willow trees, this promenade is the perfect spot to wander along the banks of the Ill or relax with a picnic in the park when the weather warms. From here you can drink in views of Petite France's rows of gabled houses.
Ⓝ Tram B: Altwinmärik

CULTURE

Cave des Hospices Civils

Go underground to the vaults of Strasbourg's oldest wine cellar, founded in 1395. During the Middle Ages, the cavernous cellar was run by a hospice who stored wine here to give to the poor, sick and needy – wine was seen as a cure for all ills. A visit to the cellars is a fascinating insight into Strasbourg's history. Look out for the world's oldest wine in a barrel, dating back to 1472, and the Theatrum Anatomicum where Goethe practised dissection.
ⓐ 1 pl. de l'Hôpital ⓣ 03 88 11 64 50 Ⓛ 08.30–12.00, 13.30–17.30 Mon–Fri, 09.00–12.30 Sat Ⓝ Tram A: Porte de l'Hôpital

La Choucrouterie

A sauerkraut factory until the 1980s, this original venue stages improvised plays, cabaret, political satire, *chanson*, mime and slapstick. Off the beaten tourist track, the intimate theatre entertains with two-hour performances in French and Alsatian that take place simultaneously with the same actors. Even if you don't speak either of these languages, it's worth a peek for its unique atmosphere. Be sure to sample the restaurant's legendary sauerkraut. ⓐ 20 rue de Saint-Louis

> **IT'S ALL IN THE NAME …**
> As you weave through Petite France's warren of narrow cobbled streets, keep an eye out for the colourful flags strung between the half-timbered houses, which represent the trades of past residents. Names to look out for include *tanneurs* (tanners), *pelletiers* (furriers), *marchands de vin* (wine merchants), *jardiniers* (gardeners) and *chasseurs* (hunters). Most of the gabled houses in this district date back to the 16th and 17th centuries. You'll notice that many of them have tall sloping roofs with open attics, which is where the tanners used to hang their skins to dry.

🕿 03 88 36 07 28 Ⓦ www.choucrouterie.com 🕘 On tour July
Ⓝ Tram A: Porte de l'Hôpital

Musée d'Art Moderne et Contemporain (Museum of Modern Art)
An immense glass-and-steel structure, Strasbourg's newcomer to the art scene is the light-flooded Museum of Modern Art on the River Ill's left bank. A Mecca to contemporary art buffs, the gallery's superb permanent collection features masterpieces by the likes of Monet, Picasso, Kandinsky, Magritte, Ernst and Sarkis. Stepping chronologically from Impressionism to Fauvism and Surrealism, the museum houses a mix of paintings, photographs, sculptures and installations. Temporary exhibitions complement the offering. ⓐ 1 pl. Hans Jean Arp 🕿 03 88 23 31 31 🕘 12.00–19.00 Tues–Sat (until 21.00 Thur), 10.00–18.00 Sun Ⓝ Tram B: Musée d'Art Moderne. Admission charge

RETAIL THERAPY

Ceramique Potter around this rustic workshop to find quality Alsatian stoneware, from chunky hand-thrown pots to snazzy eggcups. ⓐ 32 rue du Bain aux Plantes ⓣ 03 88 33 59 54 ⓛ 10.00–19.30 Wed–Sun ⓝ Tram A: Grand Rue

Un Noël en Alsace If you wish it could be Christmas every day, this glittering shop kitted out like Santa's grotto could be just the ticket. Pick up carved nativity scene figures and shiny baubles in this year-round winter wonderland. ⓐ 10 rue des Dentelles ⓣ 03 88 32 32 32 ⓦ www.noelenalsace.fr ⓛ 10.30–12.30, 13.30–18.00 Mon–Sat, 14.00–18.00 Sun, Jan–Nov; 10.00–19.00 Dec ⓝ Tram A: Grand Rue

Pain d'Epices Mireille Oster's secret recipe has won her awards and the title of 'gingerbread fairy'. From heart-shaped to almond-filled edible creations, you'll find her entire sweet selection in this white-walled store where golden cherubs shine down. ⓐ 14 rue des Dentelles ⓣ 03 88 32 33 34 ⓦ www.paindesoleil.com ⓛ 09.00–19.00 ⓝ Tram A: Grand Rue

TAKING A BREAK

L'Appart' à Tartes £ ❶ Creaking wood floors, red leather sofas and retro furniture set the scene in this funky café with a relaxed feel. A few euros will buy you a small feast of quiches, cakes and tarts. ⓐ 9 rue des Dentelles ⓣ 03 88 23 68 09

Ⓦ www.lappartatartes.com Ⓛ 12.30–14.30, 18.30–22.00 Tues–Fri, 12.00–22.00 Sat Ⓝ Tram A: Grand Rue

Art Café £ ❷ The huge Aki Kuroda fresco raises eyebrows in this contemporary, vibrant café set in the Museum of Modern Art. Enjoy a fresh salad on the terrace affording sweeping views of the River Ill. Ⓐ 1 pl. Hans Jean Arp Ⓣ 03 88 22 18 88 Ⓛ 11.00–22.00 Tues–Sun, summer; 11.00–19.00 Tues–Sun, winter Ⓝ Tram B: Musée d'Art Moderne

Chez Cat'sy £ ❸ Low beams, warm tones and soft lighting shape this cosy restaurant, where Cat'sy favourites like onion soup, Alsatian herrings and beef hotpot will make you purr. Ⓐ 22 rue des Moulins Ⓣ 03 88 21 92 33 Ⓛ 12.00–14.00, 18.30–23.00 Thur–Tues Ⓝ Tram A: Grand Rue

La Petite Venise £ ❹ A snippet of Venice awaits you at this Italian bistro with pocket-pleasing prices, where you can lunch on freshly baked Sicilian pizza, pasta and fish dishes. Ⓐ 20 rue des Moulins Ⓣ 03 88 22 66 18 Ⓛ 11.30–14.30, 18.30–22.00 Ⓝ Tram A: Grand Rue

Au Pont Saint-Martin £ ❺ Geraniums and creeping vines add a splash of colour to this attractive half-timbered building. The canal-side terrace is the place to enjoy *flammekueche* and baked camembert with a nice glass of Riesling. Ⓐ 15 rue des Moulins Ⓣ 03 88 32 45 13 Ⓦ www.pont-saint-martin.com Ⓛ 11.30–22.30 Ⓝ Tram A: Grand Rue

La Tinta £ ❻ Words, words, words... this café is obsessed with them. Here letters run up the stairs and cover the walls. Artists, poets and other well-read types gather here for strong coffee, tasty brownies and literary inspiration. ❷ 36 rue du Bain aux Plantes ❶ 03 88 32 27 94 ❺ 14.30–18.00 Mon, 10.00–18.00 Tues–Sat ❼ Tram A: Grand Rue

⬤ *La Tinta, literary café and intellectuals' haunt*

L'Escale aux Quais ££ ❼ The freshest local produce lands
on your plate at this convivial restaurant. Innovative flavours
include sauerkraut samosas and veal drenched in beer sauce.
The lunchtime *menu du jour* offers excellent value. ⓐ 2 quai
Finkwiller ❶ 03 88 37 32 34 ⓦ www.escale-aux-quais.com
🕓 19.30–22.00 Mon & Sat, 12.00–14.00, 19.30–22.00 Tues–Fri
Ⓝ Tram A: Grand Rue

AFTER DARK

RESTAURANTS

Ali Baba £ ❽ Blink and you might miss this tiny restaurant,
where the friendly owner whips up well-prepared Tunisian
cuisine. Enter the cave-like den, decorated with red-and-gold
cushions, to feast on lamb couscous with Algerian wine.
ⓐ 20 rue Finkwiller ❶ 03 88 36 05 27 🕓 12.00–15.00,
19.00–00.00 Ⓝ Tram A: Grand Rue

Fink' Stuebel £ ❾ This charming *winstub* is a real find. Dark
wood and checked tablecloths create a cosy setting to munch
on Alsatian dishes like snails and onion tart with a pitcher of
fruity Pinot Gris. Fair prices and friendly service are part and
parcel of the experience. ⓐ 26 rue Finkwiller ❶ 03 88 25 07 57
ⓦ http://finkstuebel.free.fr 🕓 12.00–14.00, 19.00–23.00
Tues–Sat Ⓝ Tram A: Grand Rue

Le Mirage £ ❿ Leopard-skin seats and oriental rugs glam
up this tiny restaurant, serving Moroccan specialities from
tasty couscous to tender lamb. ⓐ 10 Petite Rue des Dentelles

☎ 03 88 52 02 91 🕐 11.00–14.30, 19.00–00.00 Ⓝ Tram A: Grand Rue

Le Thomasien £ ⓫ Exposed stone and beams create a cosy feel in this traditional Alsatian haunt. Pull up a chair to tuck into hearty local fare such as perfectly crisp *flammekueche* and tender veal. When the sun's out, sit on the terrace. ⓐ 12 rue des Dentelles ☎ 03 88 32 76 67 🕐 12.00–14.30, 18.00–22.00 Wed–Fri, 12.00–22.00 Sat & Sun Ⓝ Tram A: Grand Rue

L'Ami Schutz ££ ⓬ Dine on one of Strasbourg's most picturesque terraces overlooking the Covered Bridges. This inviting restaurant mixes Alsatian staples like pork knuckles braised in beer schnapps with Mediterranean flavours like gazpacho and crayfish salad. ⓐ 1 Ponts Couverts ☎ 03 88 32 76 98 Ⓦ www.ami-schutz.com 🕐 11.45–13.45, 18.45–22.45 Ⓝ Tram B: Altwinmärik

La Cambuse ££ ⓭ Savour delicious seafood in this nautical-themed restaurant decked out like a ship with portholes, a wave-shaped ceiling and brass lanterns. A fusion of Provençale and Asian flavours, the imaginative menu includes specialities like herring millefeuille and dorado in curry sauce. ⓐ 1 rue des Dentelles ☎ 03 88 22 10 22 🕐 12.00–14.30, 19.00–22.30 Tues–Sat Ⓝ Tram A: Grand Rue

La Choucrouterie ££ ⓮ Got a craving for sauerkraut? Satisfy it at this former *choucrouterie* (sauerkraut factory). Tucked away down a side street, this weird but wonderful *winstub* has bags of character and a permanent whiff of vinegar. Stone walls, beaded lights and an old piano scream shabby chic and the vibe is laid back. Try the classic Alsatian sauerkraut or varieties with smoked duck and trout. 20 rue de Saint Louis 03 88 36 52 87 www.choucrouterie.com 18.30–23.00 Mon–Sat Tram A: Porte de l'Hôpital

La Maison des Tanneurs ££ 15 Formerly a tannery, this black-and-white half-timbered building beside the canal is one of Strasbourg's most beautiful. Sitting on more than 400 years of history, the wood-panelled restaurant whets appetites with Alsatian fare like garlicky snails, goose liver and *kougelhopf* cake. 42 rue du Bain aux Plantes 03 88 32 79 70 www.maison-des-tanneurs.com 12.00–14.00, 19.00–21.45 Tues–Sat Tram B: Altwinmärik

BARS & CLUBS

Académie de la Bière If you've got beer on the brain, this perennial favourite will push the right buttons. Warm wood and exposed beams create a homely feel at this popular pub, serving 200 different types of beer including Belgian Trappist brews. Tasty bar snacks are available till 03.00. 17 rue Adolphe Seyboth 03 88 22 38 88 11.00–04.00 Tram B: Altwinmärik

Au Bureau Hemmed in by chestnut trees and lofty gables, this cheery Irish pub has a shady terrace next to the River Ill. Pull up a chair to study the arm-long list of beers including Irish, Belgian, Mexican and Alsatian varieties. 2 pl. Benjamin Zix 03 88 75 15 80 11.00–01.30 Mon–Sat, 11.00–19.00 Sun Tram A: Grand Rue

Coco Lobo Ay, ay, ay! This Spanish bar decorated with bull-shaped lights and sombreros spices up the after-dark offer in Petite France. Come here to sip mojitos, nibble tapas and sway to Latin grooves. ⓐ 2 rue des Glacières ⓣ 03 88 36 12 93 ⓛ 19.00–03.30 Tues–Sat ⓝ Tram A: Grand Rue

Entre Deux With barely enough room to swing a cat, this small and friendly bar next to Ali Baba is a relaxed local haunt. ⓐ 22 rue Finkwiller ⓣ 06 50 49 99 53 ⓛ 08.00–01.30 Mon–Sat ⓝ Tram A: Grand Rue

Frog in Bar Look up to spy rugby boots dangling from the ceiling at this hole-in-the-wall bar, where cheap drinks and big-screen sports are on tap. ⓐ 28 rue Finkwiller ⓣ 03 88 14 05 95 ⓛ 11.00–01.30 Mon–Sat ⓝ Tram A: Grand Rue

Krutenau & University District

Grand Ile has got the mind-boggling cathedral, Petite France the beautiful canals, but Krutenau captures you with lesser-known charms and urban edge. Hip, young and innovative, this is the playground of the city's 50,000 students. The cityscape here is punctuated with grand turn-of-the-century townhouses, tower blocks and riverside warehouses. It may not be as pretty as the old town, but it certainly packs a punch.

Whether you want quirky boutiques or gorgeous gardens, world flavours or interactive museums, this is the place to come. Krutenau also scores points for its lively nightlife. From bars with mellow music and a boho vibe to funky clubs that raise the roof with R 'n' B beats, party-goers need look no further.

SIGHTS & ATTRACTIONS

Jardin Botanique (Botanical Gardens)

An oasis of calm, the university's peaceful botanical gardens appeal to those seeking solace from the centre's crowds. The gardens nurture around 6,000 species including cactuses, palms and rhododendrons. Fanning out from the arboretum, trails weave past monkey puzzle trees, cypress trees and Calabrian pines. There is a garden dedicated to alpine species and Alsatian vines. Rest on the boardwalk beside the lily pond.

ⓐ 28 rue Goethe ⓣ 03 90 24 18 65 ⓞ 08.00–19.30 Mon–Fri, 10.00–19.30 Sat & Sun, summer; 08.00–12.00, 14.00–16.00 Mon–Fri, 14.00–16.00 Sat & Sun, winter ⓝ Tram C: Observatoire

Parc de la Citadelle

Roam the city's ramparts at this pocket of greenery by the River Ill. The impressive fortifications complete with moat are the remains of the citadel Vauban built here in 1681. Today locals come here to cycle, jog, stroll and picnic by the water's edge.

⊘ Tram C: Esplanade

◓ *The Botanical Gardens offer a tranquil refuge from the city*

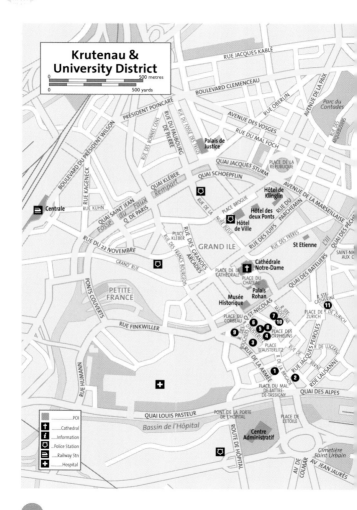

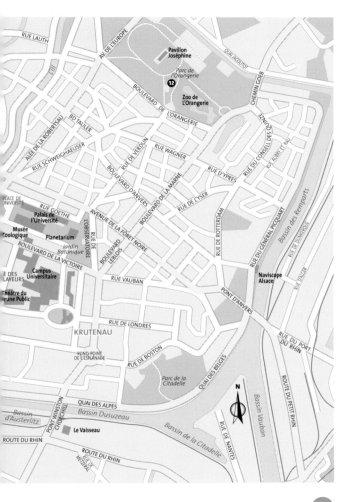

RUE LAUTH

AV DE L'EUROPE

Pavillon
Joséphine

Parc de
l'Orangerie

12

QUAI JACOUTOT

CHEMIN GOEB

Zoo de
L'Orangerie

BOULEVARD DE L'ORANGERIE

BD TAULER

ALÉE DE LA ROBERTSAU

RUE SCHWEIGHAEUSER

RUE DE VERDUN

RUE WAGNER

BOULEVARD D'ANVERS

BOULEVARD DE LA MARNE

RUE D'YPRES

RUE DU CONSEIL DES QUINZE

RUE AUBRY ET RAU

PLACE DE
L'UNIVERSITÉ

RUE GOETHE

Palais de
l'Université

Musée
Zoologique

Planetarium

Jardin
Botanique

RUE DE
L'OBSERVATOIRE

AVENUE DE LA FORÊT-NOIRE

BOULEVARD LEBLOIS

RUE DE L'YSER

RUE DE ROTTERDAM

RUE DU GÉNÉRAL PICQUART

Bassin des Remparts

RUE DE BUNKEROUE

BOULEVARD DE LA VICTOIRE

RUE DE NÉROTTERDAM

E DES
LAVEURS

Campus
Universitaire

RUE VAUBAN

Naviscope
Alsace

RUE DUCER

Théâtre du
Jeune Public

PONT D'ANVERS

RUE DE LONDRES

KRUTENAU

RUE DU PORT
DU RHIN

ROND-POINT
DE L'ESPLANADE

RUE DE BOSTON

Parc de la
Citadelle

QUAI DES BELGES

N

ROUTE DU PETIT RHIN

Bassin
d'Austerlitz

QUAI DES ALPES

Bassin Dusuzeau

Le Vaisseau

PONT WINSTON
CHURCHILL

Bassin Vauban

RUE DE NANTES

Bassin de la Citadelle

ROUTE DU RHIN

ROUTE DU RHIN

RUE DE
MÉZERAL

Parc de l'Orangerie

Green-fingered Le Nôtre who designed the gardens of Versailles also put his stamp on this beautiful park opposite the Council of Europe. Explore the chestnut tree-lined avenues and manicured formal gardens fringed with clipped bushes and flower beds that are a riot of pink and purple in summer. The focal point of the park is the lake with its dancing fountain and humpback bridges. As you wander through the gardens, look out for the pavilion built for Empress Josephine. ☎ 03 88 45 51 60 Ⓝ Bus 6, 30: Orangerie

Place de l'Université

This monumental square is a reminder of the city's 19th-century might. Slender Doric columns and arches shape the Palais Universitaire – peek inside to glimpse the lavish main hall. Opposite, there's a park framed by plane trees and peppered with fountains where students hang out in summer. Glimpse the statue dedicated to famous author and philosopher Goethe, who studied here in the late 18th century. Ⓝ Tram C: Universités

Planetarium

Stargazers head for the planetarium and observatory in the botanical gardens, capped with a huge silver dome and featuring France's third biggest astronomical telescope. Trace the movement of the planets at one of the hour-long shows, or take a tour of the dome, observatory and glittering vault of stars. ⓐ Rue de l'Observatoire ☎ 03 90 24 24 50 Ⓦ http://planetarium.u-strasbg.fr ⏱ 09.00–12.00, 14.00–17.00 Mon, Tues, Thur & Fri, 14.00–18.00 Wed & Sun, school term time; 10.00–12.15, 13.30–16.30 Mon–Fri,

14.00–17.30 Sun, school holiday time  Tram C: Observatoire. Admission charge

Zoo de l'Orangerie

Look up to spy storks flying overhead as you enter this small zoo set in the grounds of the Parc de l'Orangerie. Opened in 1895, the zoo is free and home to around 70 different species including lemurs, llamas, Siberian lynx, emus and Cretan mountain goats. Children enjoy the animal petting area. ⓐ Parc de l'Orangerie ⓘ 03 88 61 62 88 ⓝ Bus 6, 30: Orangerie

ⓐ *The leafy avenues around the university*

CULTURE

Musée Zoologique (Zoological Museum)

Budding zoologists make a beeline for this museum, showcasing one of the richest collections in France. On display are more than a million insects, thousands of mammals, fish and reptiles, including rare and extinct species. ⓐ 29 blvd de la Victoire ⓣ 03 90 24 04 85 ⓛ 12.00–18.00 Mon–Fri, 10.00–18.00 Sat & Sun ⓝ Tram C: Universités. Admission charge

Naviscope Alsace

This ship-shape museum housed in a tugboat moored on the River Ill unravels the history of Strasbourg's waterways. There's a small, intimate collection of old snapshots, model ships and anchors, plus views of the river from the top deck. Take a break in the boat's café. ⓐ 18 rue du Général Picquart ⓣ 03 88 60 22 23 ⓛ 14.30–17.30 Tues, Wed, Sat & Sun ⓝ Bus: 2, 15. Admission charge

Théâtre du Jeune Public

Moving from the Peking Opera to puppetry, comedy, mime, musicals and circus-inspired performance, this theatre's eclectic repertoire is geared towards the young and young at heart. Housed in a grand 19th-century building, the cultural venue blends tried-and-tested favourites with experimental works for tots to teens. ⓐ 7 rue des Balayeurs ⓣ 03 88 35 70 10 ⓦ www.theatre-jeune-public.com ⓝ Tram C: Universités

Le Vaisseau

Discover your inner child at this interactive museum beside

THE STORKS OF STRASBOURG

From shop signs to cuddly toys, pretty much everywhere you look in Strasbourg you'll see the city's beloved bird: the stork. The symbol of Alsace, the migratory stork used to be a common sight when it arrived in spring, but numbers have declined over recent years. Conservation efforts are now being made to increase the stork population – for instance, at Steinbourg's Stork Reintegration Centre near Saverne and the Zoo de l'Orangerie where you can take a closer look at these long-legged birds.

The famed carrier of newborn babies in bundles, the stork represents fertility and joy. If you want to spot them, make sure you fix your gaze to the skies where they soar and build nests in high places. You're more likely to see than hear them – they are mute and communicate by bill-clattering.

the river, where kids of all ages can let off steam. The open-plan museum with an educational twist features plenty of hands-on displays offering hours of fun, from climbing larger-than-life spider webs to blowing enormous bubbles and presenting the news live on air. Highlights include flying the magic carpet, creating cartoons using sound effects and slithering through a tunnel teeming with ants. ⓐ 1 bis rue Philippe Dollinger ⓣ 03 88 44 44 00 ⓦ www.levaisseau.com ⓛ 10.00–18.00 Tues–Sun ⓝ Tram C: Esplanade. Admission charge

RETAIL THERAPY

L'Art du Vin Gleaming bottles line the walls at this intoxicating little shop, where home-grown varieties like Pinot Gris and Riesling share shelf space with world wines. 🅰 16 rue d'Austerlitz ☎ 03 88 35 12 28 🕐 09.00–12.30, 14.00–19.00 🚊 Tram A: Porte de l'Hôpital

Litzler Vogel Row upon row of picture-perfect pralines, bonbons and truffles tempt you to loosen your purse strings at this smart *patisserie* and *chocolatier*. The marzipan animals, cognac truffles and almond pralines are edible works of art. 🅰 9 rue d'Austerlitz ☎ 03 88 36 21 77 🕐 08.00–19.00 Tues–Fri, 07.30–19.00 Sat, 07.30–16.30 Sun, winter; 07.30–13.30 Sun, summer 🚊 Tram A: Porte de l'Hôpital

Panier des Pâtes Foodies bag fine Alsatian and Italian specialities from ravioli to pesto and tiramisu at this dinky shop. 🅰 7 rue d'Austerlitz ☎ 03 88 25 53 59 🕐 10.00–14.00, 15.30–19.00 Tues–Fri, 10.00–14.00, 15.30–18.00 Sat 🚊 Tram A: Porte de l'Hôpital

Signe du Temps Fashionistas sniff out the latest styles at this trendy boutique with urban flavour. 🅰 8 rue Sainte-Madeleine ☎ 03 88 25 54 50 🕐 10.00–12.00, 14.00–19.00 Tues–Sat 🚊 Tram A: Porte de l'Hôpital

TAKING A BREAK

Brasserie de la Bourse £ ❶ Kick back in the comfy armchairs of this classic French brasserie in a Belle Époque building. The fixed lunch menu offers value. Expect staples like *flammekueche* and sauerkraut. **ⓐ** 1 pl. du Mal de-Lattre-de-Tassigny **ⓣ** 03 88 36 40 53 **ⓛ** 12.00–14.30, 18.30–23.00 **Ⓝ** Tram A: Étoile Bourse

Brasserie Stern £ ❷ Cartoon images and huge mirrors grace the red walls in this modern, relaxed café serving decent breakfasts and good espresso with crêpes. **ⓐ** 3 rue de la Brigade **ⓣ** 03 88 36 62 38 **ⓛ** 07.00–22.00 Mon–Sat, 10.00-19.00 Sun **Ⓝ** Tram A: Étoile Bourse

Chez Michel £ ❸ *Moules et frites* (mussels and chips) are the speciality of this no-frills restaurant kitted out with brick walls

🔺 *Pretzel stand, Krutenau*

and wood panelling. There are plenty of varieties to choose from.
ⓐ 8 rue d'Austerlitz ☎ 03 88 25 17 66 ⏰ 12.00–13.30, 19.00–22.00
Mon, Tues, Thur & Sat Ⓝ Tram A: Porte de l'Hôpital

Nicolas £ ❹ Pause for coffee with chocolate éclairs, apple tart or
handmade pralines at this cosy *pâtisserie* and tea room. There's
a small terrace where you can rest your feet. ⓐ 17 rue d'Austerlitz
☎ 03 88 36 19 81 ⏰ 07.30–19.00 Tues–Sun Ⓝ Tram A: Porte
de l'Hôpital

Rémy et Jimmy £ ❺ Ice cream tastes divine on the terrace of
this French ice cream parlour. Cool down with homemade
peach, pistachio and fresh fruit varieties. ⓐ 3 rue d'Austerlitz
☎ 03 88 14 08 09 ⏰ 12.00–00.00 Mon, 08.00–00.00 Tues–Sun,
summer; 12.00–19.00 Mon, 08.00–19.00 Tues–Sun, winter
Ⓝ Tram A: Porte de l'Hôpital

AFTER DARK

RESTAURANTS

Au Canon £ ❻ This bistro's buzzing terrace looks inviting, but
it's worth taking a peek inside. Decked out with a spectacular
skylight and black-and-white photos of old Strasbourg, this 18th-
century building crammed with curiosities is where Alsace's
first beer was brewed. ⓐ 1 pl. du Corbeau ☎ 03 88 37 06 39
⏰ 07.00–22.00 Ⓝ Tram A: Porte de l'Hôpital

La Coccinelle £ ❼ This traditional *winstub* called 'The Ladybird'
knocks spots off many others. The lantern-lit restaurant serves

hearty local favourites like *pot au feu* (stew) and Alsatian snails by the half dozen with zesty Pinot Blanc. ⓐ 22 rue Sainte-Madeleine ⓣ 03 88 36 19 27 ⓛ 12.00–14.00, 19.00–22.00 Mon–Fri, 19.00–22.00 Sat ⓣ Tram A: Porte de l'Hôpital

Au Grain de Riz £ ❽ If you've had your fill of Alsatian fare and are seeking a little spice, this pocket-sized restaurant comes up with the goods. Feast on Lao flavours from papaya salad to Mekong fish. ⓐ 5A rue d'Austerlitz ⓣ 03 88 35 57 57 ⓛ 12.00–15.00, 19.00–00.00 Tues–Sat, 19.00–00.00 Sun ⓣ Tram A: Porte de l'Hôpital

Kashmir £ ❾ Fiery biryanis and red-hot madras curries are on the menu at this authentic and value-for-money Indian restaurant. ⓐ 2 rue des Bouchers ⓣ 03 88 25 18 08 ⓛ 12.00–14.00, 18.30–23.00 Mon–Sat, 18.30–23.00 Sun ⓣ Tram A: Porte de l'Hôpital

Au Potiron £ ❿ Vegetarians make for this cheery home-grown restaurant, dishing up freshly baked pizzas using organic ingredients. The prices are pretty appetising too. ⓐ 24 rue Sainte-Madeleine ⓣ 03 88 35 49 86 ⓛ 12.00–14.00, 19.00–22.30 Mon–Sat ⓣ Tram A: Porte de l'Hôpital

Wo d'Fuchs zu de Gänze Predigt £ ⓫ Savour game at this rustic, 16th-century restaurant where the chef doubles as a hunter. Creaking beams, wall paintings and red lamps create a homely feel. ⓐ 34 rue de Zurich ⓣ 03 88 35 62 87 ⓛ 12.00–14.00, 19.00–22.00 Mon–Fri, 19.00–22.00 Sat & Sun ⓣ Tram A: Porte de l'Hôpital

Buerehiesel £££ ⓬ Behind the blushing bricks of this gingerbready house in the Parc de l'Orangerie is one of Strasbourg's top gastro haunts. Crowned with three Michelin stars, this is where master chef Antoine Westermann cooks up specialities like slow-cooked Bresse chicken and Alsatian pigeon. ⓐ 4 parc de l'Orangerie ⓣ 03 88 45 56 65 ⓦ www.buerehiesel.fr ⓛ 12.00–14.00, 19.30–22.00 Tues–Sat ⓝ Bus 6, 30: Orangerie

BARS & CLUBS

Bar C4 Psychedelic lamps and turquoise tub chairs set the scene at this lively bar, where DJs spin on the decks and bar staff whip up superb cocktails. ⓐ 9 quai des Pêcheurs ⓣ 03 88 24 04 34 ⓛ 21.30–03.00 Tues–Thur, 21.00–04.00 Fri & Sat ⓝ Tram C: Universités

Giraf'Café At the hip heart of Krutenau, this little bar reels in a mixed bunch that come for the Danish Giraf beer, mellow vibes and fair prices. ⓐ 6 pl. Saint-Nicolas aux Ondes ⓣ 03 88 14 06 06 ⓛ 11.00–04.00 ⓝ Tram C: Universités

---

● *The characteristic painted buildings of Colmar old town*

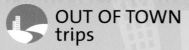

Colmar

With its wistful spires, half-timbered houses and flower-strewn canals, Colmar is a dreamy corner of Alsace. Whether you're sipping *café au lait* in Little Venice, listening to accordion players by the Maison des Têtes, or wandering the lantern-lit backstreets by night, it's hard not to be enchanted by this place.

Colmar is big enough to have magnificent churches, gourmet restaurants, designer shopping and superb museums, yet still small enough to discover on foot. Fine foie gras and gondolas, Pinot Noir and Picasso, this place tastes as good as it looks.

For details of Colmar's tourist office, see page 136.

△ *Colmar's half-timbered buildings are straight out of a fairytale*

GETTING THERE

Situated 75 km (47 miles) south of Strasbourg, Colmar takes under an hour to reach on the A35 motorway. The town is easily accessible by public transport, with a frequent train service linking Strasbourg to Colmar in about 30 minutes.
SNCF 🛈 08 92 35 35 35 🌐 www.ter-sncf.com

SIGHTS & ATTRACTIONS

Collégiale Saint-Martin (St Martin's Church)

Punctured spires, filigree stonework and a mosaic-tiled roof shape this beautiful Gothic church. Glimpse grimacing gargoyles and the colourful clock face on the façade. Step inside to admire cross-ribbed vaulting and stained glass. ⓐ Pl. de la Cathédrale
🛈 03 89 41 27 20 🕓 08.00–19.00 May–Oct; 08.00–18.30 Nov–Apr
🚌 Bus 7: Hôtel de Ville

Église des Dominicains (Dominican Church)

Built on eighth-century foundations, this vast sandstone edifice is an oasis of calm in the centre and shelters Martin Schongauer's well-known Virgin of the Rosebush, depicting the Virgin and Child in a garden of roses. ⓐ Pl. des Dominicains
🛈 03 89 24 46 57 🕓 10.00–13.00, 15.00–18.00 🚌 Bus 7: Hôtel de Ville. Admission charge

Maison Martin Jund

There's no need to venture out of Colmar to sample wine straight from the barrel. This family-run winery dating back

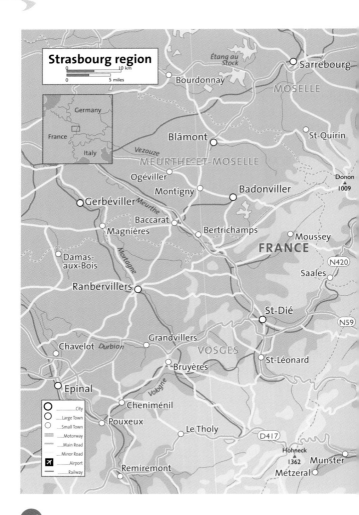

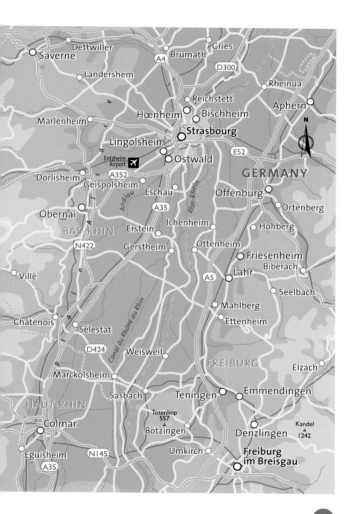

to 1603 produces fine wines from Edelzwicker and Pinot Blanc to Riesling and Sylvaner. Before you taste the grape, take a tour of the cellar to hear the gurgle of filling barrels. ⓐ 12 rue de l'Ange ⓣ 03 89 41 58 72 ⓦ www.martinjund.com ⓛ 09.00–12.00, 14.00–18.00 ⓝ Bus 7: Hôtel de Ville

Maison Pfister

With its wooden loggia and turrets, this Renaissance gem built for wealthy hatter Ludwig Scherer in 1537 is one of Colmar's most striking townhouses. Although the frescoes are a little faded, on closer inspection you'll see they represent allegorical figures, biblical scenes and German emperors. ⓐ Rue Mercière ⓝ Bus 7: Ancienne Douane

Maison des Têtes (House of Heads)

Feel like someone is watching you? It'll be the heads festooned over the façade of this house with stepped gables, built for merchant Anton Burger in 1609. From laughing jesters to pious monks and eerie ghouls, the heads never fail to raise eyebrows. Crowning the roof is Bartholdi's statue of an Alsatian barrel maker, a reminder of the wine exchange once housed here. ⓐ 19 rue des Têtes ⓝ Bus 7: Hôtel de Ville

Petite Venise (Little Venice)

It's fair to say that, while all of Colmar is pretty, the Little Venice district wins first prize in the beauty contest with its candy-coloured houses, cobbled streets and picturesque canals. Take a stroll here to spot lofty half-timbered houses, stone bridges hung heavy with flower baskets and alleyways so narrow you can touch either side. In summer, explore the waterways on a 30-minute boat tour. Boat tours: ⓐ 12A rue de la Herse ⓣ 03 89 41 01 94 ⓦ www.sweetnarcisse.com ⓛ 10.00–12.00, 13.30–19.00 Apr–Sept ⓝ Bus 7: Six Montagnes Noires

Place de l'Ancienne Douane

Hemmed in by half-timbered houses, this square is at its most impressive by night when the Ancienne Douane (Old Custom House) is illuminated. Dating back to 1480, the fairytale building features a mosaic-tiled roof, loggia and tower overlooking the attractive Schwendi fountain. ⓝ Bus 7: Ancienne Douane

● *The eerie House of Heads* (Maison des Têtes)

CULTURE

Musée Bartholdi (Bartholdi Museum)

This 18th-century town mansion is the birthplace of Frédéric Auguste Bartholdi, creator of the Statue of Liberty. Tracing the life and works of this famous sculptor, the intriguing museum houses a peerless collection of his models, bronze sculptures, watercolours and oil paintings. Family heirlooms give the museum a personal touch. ⓐ 30 rue des Marchands ❶ 03 89 41 90 60 ⓦ www.musee-bartholdi.com ❶ 10.00–12.00, 14.00–18.00 Wed–Mon ⓝ Bus 7: Ancienne Douane. Admission charge

Musée d'Histoire Naturelle et d'Ethnographie (Natural History and Ethnography Museum)

If you're mad about minerals, pre-Columbian pottery and Egyptian mummies, unearth a treasure trove of ancient artefacts, rocks and endangered animals in this museum near

FOLLOW YOUR NOSE …

Colmar lies at the heart of the 170 km (106 mile) **Route des Vins d'Alsace** (Alsatian Wine Route, ⓦ www.alsace-route-des-vins.com), featuring wineries that offer rich pickings. If you're into wine, it's worth hiring a car to explore this route, with its gently rolling vineyards, picturesque villages and medieval castles. Take a stroll through the vines or taste the produce in local *winstubs*.

Little Venice. @ 11 rue Turenne ☎ 03 89 23 84 15 ⏱ 10.00–12.00, 14.00–17.00 Wed–Mon ⊗ Bus 7: Krutenau. Admission charge

Musée d'Unterlinden (Unterlinden Museum)

Housed in a former Dominican convent with a lovely Gothic cloister, this museum is the highlight of a visit to Colmar. Must-sees include Mathias Grünewald's 16th-century Issenheim altar-piece (one of the most precious works of European art of that age) and the Bergheim mosaic. Pause to admire medieval and Renaissance pieces, Gothic sculpture, decorative arts and modern masterpieces from the likes of Monet, Picasso and Dix. @ 1 rue d'Unterlinden ☎ 03 89 20 15 50 ⓦ www.musee-unterlinden.com ⏱ 09.00–18.00 May–Oct; 09.00–12.00, 14.00–17.00 Wed–Mon, Nov–Apr ⊗ Bus 1: Unterlinden. Admission charge

RETAIL THERAPY

Choco en Têtes The aroma of cocoa drifts from this mouth-watering shop, where arty pralines from pumpkins and hedgehogs to shiny chocolate conkers fill the window. You can also buy gingerbread by the slice, chocolate stork eggs and handcrafted nutcrackers here. @ 7 rue des Têtes ☎ 03 89 24 35 02 ⏱ 14.00–18.30 Mon, 10.00–12.00, 14.00–18.30 Tues–Sat ⊗ Bus 7: Hôtel de Ville

Les Foies Gras de Liesel Foie gras lovers should make for this gourmet store, where Marco Willmann shows pride and passion in providing some of Alsace's finest duck and goose foie. Based on a secret recipe, the foie gras here is the best money can buy.

ⓐ 3 rue Turenne ⓣ 03 89 23 88 29 ⓦ www.alsacefoiegras.com
ⓛ 09.30–12.30, 15.00–19.00 Tues–Sat ⓝ Bus 7: Six Montagnes Noires

Sézanne This speciality store is brimming with regional produce from potted rabbit with prunes to Alsatian honey, mustard chutney and gingerbread. Pop down to the cellar for local wines. ⓐ 30 Grand Rue ⓣ 03 89 41 55 94 ⓛ 09.00–19.00, July & Aug; 09.00–19.00 Mon–Sat, Sept–June ⓝ Bus 7: Ancienne Douane

TAKING A BREAK

Café de France £ Warm and low lit, this quintessential French brasserie opposite the Maison des Têtes is decked out with portraits of famous French actors and musicians. The daily menu offers excellent value. ⓐ 20 rue des Têtes ⓣ 03 89 24 55 42 ⓛ 08.00–22.00 ⓝ Bus 7: Hôtel de Ville

Crêpe Stub £ A great budget option, this dinky café is the place to try homemade onion tart and perfect chocolate crêpes for very little. ⓐ 10 rue des Tanneurs ⓣ 03 89 24 51 88 ⓛ 11.30–14.00, 18.30–22.00 Fri–Wed ⓝ Bus 7: Marché aux Fruits

Au Doré £ With its art nouveau windows, bubble-gum façade and unique touches, this tiny café near the Bartholdi Museum plays French *chanson* and has bags of old-world charm. The friendly staff serve snacks like *tarte au fromage* (cheese tart) with an excellent cup of coffee. ⓐ 28 rue des Marchands ⓣ 03 89 23 70 81 ⓛ 08.00–19.30 Tues–Sun ⓝ Bus 7: Ancienne Douane

Paul £ This *pâtisserie* on one of Colmar's main shopping drags makes mouths water with freshly baked croissants, strawberry tarts and raisin brioches. **ⓐ** 62 rue des Clefs **ⓣ** 03 89 24 16 62 **ⓛ** 07.30–19.30 Mon–Fri, 07.30–19.00 Sat **ⓝ** Bus 7: Hôtel de Ville

Winstub Unterlinden ££ Opposite Unterlinden Museum, this attractive bistro has a covered terrace where you can refuel with Alsatian specialities like *flammekueche*. **ⓐ** 2 rue des Unterlinden **ⓣ** 03 89 41 18 73 **ⓦ** www.unterlinden.com **ⓛ** 11.30–22.30 **ⓝ** Bus 1: Unterlinden

AFTER DARK

RESTAURANTS

Brasserie Heydel £ With dark polished wood and low lighting, this snug French brasserie serves value-for-money menus. Try specialities like flavoursome Munster tart and *kougelhopf*. **ⓐ** 45 rue des Clefs **ⓣ** 03 89 41 54 64 **ⓦ** www.brasserie-heydel.fr **ⓛ** 08.00–00.00 Tues–Sat **ⓝ** Bus 7: Hôtel de Ville

La Krutenau £ Soak up the views of Little Venice's canals from this restaurant's terrace. Enjoy a glass of Riesling, *flammekueche* or watch boats cruising along the waterways in summer. **ⓐ** 1 rue de la Poissonerie **ⓣ** 03 89 41 18 80 **ⓛ** 10.00–00.00 **ⓝ** Bus 7: Montagnes Noires

Winstub La Petite Venise £ This chalet-style *winstub* is kitted out with *kougelhopf* cake moulds and snapshots of old Alsace. Savour hot Munster cheese salad. **ⓐ** 4 rue de la Poissonerie

☎ 03 89 41 72 59 **🕐** 19.00–21.30 Tues, 12.00–14.00, 19.00–21.30 Wed, Fri–Mon **Ⓝ** Bus 7: Montagnes Noires

La Pergola £–££ Pink pigs in all shapes and sizes reel you into this quirky restaurant, where braised ham, wiener schnitzel and pork medallions are staples on the menu. Dangling marionettes make the front of this popular restaurant feel like Geppetto's workshop. There are no fixed opening times. **ⓐ** 24 rue des Marchands **☎** 03 89 41 36 79 **Ⓝ** Bus 7: Hôtel de Ville

Restaurant Maison des Têtes ££–£££ Housed in the Maison des Têtes, this gourmet haunt opens onto a cobbled inner courtyard. Feast on delicacies like oyster with curried crayfish and veal with truffles in the wood-beamed dining room. **ⓐ** 19 rue des Têtes **☎** 03 89 24 43 43 **Ⓦ** www.maisondestetes.com **🕐** 12.00–14.00, 19.00–21.30 **Ⓝ** Bus 7: Hôtel de Ville

ACCOMMODATION

Maison Martin Jund £ Seeking somewhere original to sleep? This 17th-century winery has a range of inviting studios with kitchenettes, comfy beds and excellent views. Many feature original touches like period furniture and slanted beams. **ⓐ** 12 rue de l'Ange **☎** 03 89 41 58 72 **Ⓦ** www.martinjund.com **Ⓝ** Bus 7: Hôtel de Ville

Mittelharth AJ £ The clean dorms at this youth hostel are one of the cheapest deals in town. **ⓐ** 2 rue Pasteur **☎** 03 89 80 57 39 **Ⓝ** Bus 4, 5: Pont Rouge

Hotel Saint-Martin ££ Exposed stone walls, low beams and warm colours set the scene in this smart Alsatian-style hotel set around an inner courtyard. All rooms have satellite TV and minibar. ⓐ 38 Grand Rue ⓣ 03 89 24 11 51 ⓦ www.hotel-saint-martin.com ⓜ Bus 7: Ancienne Douane

🔺 *Authentic Alsace lodgings, Hotel Saint-Martin*

Saverne

The town of creeping roses and rambling ramparts, neat and petite Saverne is pinned to Alsace's green heart. The cobbled streets speckled with turreted palaces and half-timbered houses festooned with geraniums have a friendly and laid-back

🔺 *The Marne-Rhine Canal cuts through historic Saverne*

feel. This back-to-nature haven with a cultural twist fuses outdoor activities with sights to rival any of the biggies you care to mention.

Saverne, small enough to walk or cycle round, lies at the foothills of the Vosges mountains. On offer are picturesque walks along the banks of the Marne-Rhine Canal, peaceful botanical gardens and precipitous medieval fortresses. Once a Roman settlement called *Tres Tabernae* (Three Taverns), it has kept its historic charm and is a taste of old-world Alsace.

For details of Saverne's tourist office, see page 136. ❶ There is no public transport in Saverne itself, as it is too small. However, you will find buses running to other villages.

GETTING THERE

Located northwest of Strasbourg, Saverne is linked to the city by the speedy A4 motorway. On a clear run, the 50 km (31 mile) route takes just 30 minutes. **SNCF** (❶ 08 92 35 35 35 Ⓦ www.ter-sncf.com/alsace) operates a frequent train service to Saverne's main station, with the journey taking about 35 minutes.

SIGHTS & ATTRACTIONS

Château du Greifenstein (Greifenstein Castle)
Peering above the treetops, these ivy-clad ruins date back to the Middle Ages. Although little remains of the feudal fortress, the 12th-century keep is impressive and the atmospheric site affords sweeping views over the Zorn valley. ❸ Follow signs from Route de Paris ❶ 03 88 91 80 47 (tourist office)

Château de Haut Barr (Haut Barr Castle)

Clinging precipitously to red rocks, this ruined fortress on a steep hill has medieval roots. Dubbed the 'eye of Alsace', the crumbling ruins straddle three huge rocks. Cross the *Pont du Diable* (Devil's Bridge) for views over the Zorn valley, the plains of Alsace and the Vosges mountains. On a fine day, you'll see Strasbourg cathedral's tower and Germany's Black Forest. ⓐ Follow signs from Rue du Général Leclerc ⓣ 03 88 91 80 47 (tourist office)

Cloître des Récollets (Récollets Monastery)

Saverne's red-brick Franciscan monastery and church date back to the 14th century. Keep an eye out for the elaborate murals beneath the arches depicting biblical scenes and the sundial gracing the façade of the church. The inner courtyard's gardens surround a central fountain and are fringed by fragrant medicinal plants and herbs. ⓐ Rue Poincaré ⓣ 03 88 71 21 33 ⓛ 08.00–18.00

Jardin Botanique de Saverne (Saverne Botanical Garden)

Wander through Saverne's well-kept botanical garden to sniff out alpine species, medicinal plants and scented herbs. The tranquil garden offers rhododendrons, lilies and irises plus an orchid lawn and unusual species like carnivorous pitcher plants. ⓐ Route de Phalsbourg ⓣ 03 88 91 21 00 ⓛ 14.00–18.00 Sat & Sun, Apr & Sept; 10.00–19.00 May–Aug. Admission charge

Place de la Licorne

Be sure to glimpse Saverne's symbol – the fabled unicorn – rising like a vision on Place de la Licorne. Legend has it that

HEAVY ROCK

Jutting out of the landscape, the rocky outcrop *Saut du Prince Charles* (Prince Charles' Leap) has a story to tell. Legend has it that Prince Charles of Lorraine fled on horseback and managed to escape attack by leaping from this rock near the Route du Col de Saverne. If the hoof prints embedded in stone are anything to go by, there may be some truth in the tale.

this fantastical creature wet its horn in Badbrünne fountain, which people during medieval times believed to have healing properties.

Roseraie (Rose Garden)

Saverne's fragrant rose garden cultivates some 550 different varieties, allowing the town to compete at international level. Positively blooming during the summer, the colourful gardens give rise to pink climbers, red ramblers, apricot tea roses ... in fact, probably every rose under the sun. ⓐ Rue de la Roseraie ⓣ 03 88 71 21 33 ⓦ www.roseraie-saverne.fr ⓛ 10.00–19.00 May–Sept. Admission charge

Tour Cagliostro (Cagliostro Tower)

Look to the right of Rohan Palace (see page 120) to spot this turreted tower, where the mysterious Count of Cagliostro, alias Giuseppe Balsamo, carried out alchemy experiments and dabbled in black magic in the 18th century. This enigmatic man supposedly

had psychic powers and is said to have predicted the French Revolution. He influenced several writers including Goethe and Schiller. Pl. du Général de Gaulle

CULTURE

Château des Rohan (Rohan Palace)

A visit to Saverne's rose-hued château is a must. Once home to prince bishops, this neoclassical palace is surrounded by flower gardens and impresses with its slender columns and sculptures. The opulent palace shelters a museum in its vaults that exhibits everything from Gallo-Roman artefacts to traditional Alsatian costumes. Take a peek at the Louise Weiss collection of 20th-century paintings and decorative arts. Pl. du Général de Gaulle 03 88 91 06 28 (museum) musee.saverne@wanadoo.fr 14.00–18.00 Mon–Fri, 10.00–12.00, 14.00–18.00 Sat & Sun, Sept–June. Admission charge

Maison St-Florent

Founded by Father Libermann, a pioneer of missionary work in Africa during the 19th century, this centre houses a unique collection of African artworks including intricate funerary carvings, masks, instruments, jewellery and tools. 7 route de Paris 03 88 01 83 53 14.00–17.00 Tues, Fri & Sun

RECREATION

Océanide Relax with a long soak in effervescent waters or steam in the *hammam* and sauna at this modern leisure complex. Kids

An ancient Romanesque belfry rises over the town

love the waterslides and rapid river. ⓐ 10 rue du Centre Nautique
ⓣ 03 88 02 52 80 ⓦ www.oceanide.cc-saverne.fr ⓛ 12.00–14.00,
17.15–20.00 Mon & Tues, 10.00–20.00 Wed, 17.15–20.00 Thur,
12.00–14.00, 17.15–21.00 Fri, 10.00–12.00, 14.00–18.00 Sat,
09.00–17.00 Sun. Admission charge

Sentier Sylvicole Avid walkers don sturdy boots and make for this
forest trail just south of Saverne. The one and a half hour hike
weaves through peaceful woodlands of chestnut, fir and ancient
oak trees to Haut Barr Castle. ⓣ 03 88 91 80 47 (tourist office)

Vosges Mountains Trail Crisscrossed with well-marked
paths, Saverne is perfect two-wheel territory. Get on your
bike to cycle this 21 km (13 mile) trail at the foot of the Vosges
mountains, taking in country views and pretty Alsatian villages.
The hilly track begins in Saverne and covers highlights like
Griesbach-le-Bastberg, the famed haunt of witches and
Steinbourg's Stork Reintegration Centre. The final stretch
follows the meandering Marne-Rhine Canal back into town.
ⓣ 03 88 91 80 47 (tourist office)

RETAIL THERAPY

Le Bouton de Rose Master *chocolatier* Christian Boistelle makes
mouths water with his dark chocolate, rose-flavoured creations.
In the form of rosebuds, his famous chocolates make a unique gift
– if they last till you get home! ⓐ 92 Grand Rue ⓣ 03 88 91 10 55
ⓛ 07.00–18.30 Tues–Sat, 07.30–12.00 Sun

Jacques Bockel Rows of delectable sweets tempt at this one-stop chocolate shop. Pick up rose- or asparagus-shaped pralines filled with almonds or chocolates from around the world. ⓐ 77 Grand Rue ⓣ 03 88 02 06 78 ⓦ www.planet-chocolate.com ⓛ 14.00–18.00 Mon, 09.00–12.00, 14.00–19.00 Tues–Fri, 09.00–12.00, 14.00–18.00 Sat

Saverne Farmers' Market Shop for pungent cheeses, fresh fruit and duck foie gras at this bustling market selling produce from the region. ⓐ Pl. du Général de Gaulle ⓛ 08.00–12.00 Tues & Sat

TAKING A BREAK

La Crêpe Doré £ Satisfy your sweet tooth with pancakes and waffles with whipped cream at this crêperie in the centre of town. ⓐ 3 rue des Murs ⓣ 03 88 71 23 69 ⓛ 10.00–22.00 Mon, Tues, Thur–Sat, 10.00–14.00 Wed, 11.45–22.00 Sun

Pâtisserie Baehl £ Pause for homemade cakes, pastries, quiches and ice cream on the shady terrace of this charming tea room. ⓐ 128–130 Grand Rue ⓣ 03 88 91 12 01 ⓛ 06.30–19.00 Tues–Sun

Pâtisserie Haushalter £ Enjoy a light lunch for little at this attractive café with superb views of the blushing Rohan Palace. Do make sure you save some room for delicious chocolate gâteau or rose pastries. ⓐ 66–68 Grand Rue ⓣ 03 88 91 13 30 ⓔ info@patisseriehaushalter.fr ⓛ 07.00–19.00

⬤ *Eight out of ten cats prefer La Taverne Katz*

AFTER DARK

RESTAURANTS

Le Caveau de l'Escale £ Overlooking the marina, this vaulted restaurant whets appetites with garlicky escargots and tender veal. Pull up a chair on the terrace in summer. ⓐ 10 quai du Canal ⓣ 03 88 91 12 23 ⓦ www.escale-saverne.fr ⓛ 12.00–13.30, 19.00–21.30 Mon, Thur, Fri & Sun, 12.00–13.30 Tues, 19.00–21.30 Sat

La Taverne Katz £ Housed in Saverne's most striking half-timbered building dating back to 1605, this restaurant serves tastes of traditional Alsace. Inside, creaking beams and rich wood panelling set the scene for you to savour dishes like goose, sauerkraut and beer-braised pork. ⓐ 80 Grand Rue ⓣ 03 88 71 16 56 ⓦ www.tavernekatz.com ⓛ 12.00–14.00, 18.00–22.00

Restaurant du Château de Haut Barr ££ It's worth the climb to this gourmet haunt at the top of the hill to sample Bernard Baudendistel's homemade foie gras. You'll feel like the king of the castle in this turreted restaurant next to the ruined fortress. ⓐ Château de Haut Barr ⓣ 03 88 91 17 61 ⓔ hautbarr@free.fr ⓛ 09.00–23.00 Tues–Sun

ACCOMMODATION

AJ Saverne £ Backpackers sleep sweetly on the third floor of the 18th-century Rohan Palace. Dorms are clean and spacious, but the palatial location is the big draw. ⓐ Château des Rohan ⓣ 03 88 91 14 84 ⓦ www.fuaj.org

Camping Saverne £ This green and pleasant site is the perfect spot to pitch your tent beneath the willow trees and explore the nearby Vosges mountains. ⓐ 40 rue du Père Libermann ⓣ 03 88 91 35 65 ⓦ www.campingsaverne.com ⓛ Apr–Sept

Chez Jean ££ Floral drapes, warm hues and chunky wood furniture give this hotel's rooms a country cottage feel. Unwind in the sauna, enjoy free wireless internet, or refuel with hearty Alsatian fare in Winstub S'Rosestiebel. ⓐ 3 rue de la Gare ⓣ 03 88 91 10 19 ⓦ www.chez-jean.com

Hôtel Europe ££ Pick a room to suit your mood, from classic English to quintessential French at this 3-star hotel just a few paces from Rohan Palace. ⓐ 7 rue de la Gare ⓣ 03 88 71 12 07 ⓦ www.hotel-europe-fr.com

ⓓ *Colmar train station*

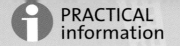

Directory

GETTING THERE

By air

Several well-known airlines (e.g. Air France) operate a frequent service between Strasbourg-Entzheim International Airport (see page 50) and destinations across Europe such as London, Amsterdam, Brussels, Madrid and Paris. The airport is a 15-minute journey from the centre and has services including ATMs, shops and bars. Ryanair offers cheap flights between London, Dublin, Rome and Barcelona and Baden Airpark in Germany (35 minutes' drive from Strasbourg).

Air Berlin ⓦ www.airberlin.com

Air France ⓦ www.airfrance.com

Ryanair ⓦ www.ryanair.com

Many people are aware that air travel emits CO_2, which contributes to climate change. You may be interested in the possibility of lessening the environmental impact of your flight through the charity **Climate Care** (ⓦ www.climatecare.org), which offsets your CO_2 by funding environmental projects around the world.

By rail

Strasbourg's expansive **main station** (ⓣ 08 92 35 35 35 ⓦ www.ter-sncf.com/alsace) on Place de la Gare is the base for regional TER and long-distance SNCF trains. There are regular, high-speed connections to French cities such as Paris, Bordeaux and Lyon, plus international destinations including Brussels, Munich and Rome.

The monthly *Thomas Cook European Rail Timetable* has up-to-date schedules for European international and national train services.

Thomas Cook European Rail Timetable ☎ (UK) 01733 416477, (USA) 1 800 322 3834 ⓦ www.thomascookpublishing.com

By road

France has an excellent road network, but do keep some change or a credit card handy when driving on *autoroutes* (motorways), as most have tolls. *Routes nationales* (A-roads) are free but can be much slower. The national speed limit on motorways is 130 kph (80 mph), with driving on the right. Try to avoid rush hour (08.00–09.30, 16.30–18.30 Mon–Fri) when roads are often congested. The **French Motorway Association** (ASFA ⓦ www.autoroutes.fr) provides the latest traffic information and detailed route maps.

Eurolines (ⓦ www.eurolines.com) pull up in front of the Citroën garage on Rue Maréchal Lefebvre. They operate a Europe-wide service to cities such as Amsterdam, Berlin, London and Vienna.

ENTRY FORMALITIES

If you are an EU, Australian, Canadian, New Zealand or US citizen, you'll need a valid passport to enter France, but not a visa for stays of less than 90 days. However, you may need a visa if you are arriving from another country. Contact your consulate or embassy before departure. The **French Ministry for Foreign Affairs** (ⓦ www.diplomatie.gouv.fr) provides more information on entry requirements.

While it's free to import goods of up to €175 from a non-EU country, you should check restrictions on importing tobacco, perfume and alcohol. More information is available at
Ⓦ www.douane.gouv.fr

MONEY

France's currency is the euro (€), broken down into 100 cents. Coins are in denominations of 1, 2, 5, 10, 20 and 50 cents, and of 1 and 2 euros. There are banknotes of 5, 10, 20, 50, 100, 200 and 500 euros.

You'll find a number of ATMs in central Strasbourg. Some are in operation 24 hours a day. Banks are normally open 08.30–12.30 and 13.30–16.30 Monday to Friday, and some open on Saturdays. Main branches like Deutsche Bank on Augustusplatz do not close for lunch.

❶ Banks tend to offer better currency exchange and traveller's cheque rates than bureaux de change. Some of the major post offices, including the one on Place du Château, can also change money. Central banks of interest to travellers include the Banque de France on Place Broglie, Barclays Bank on Place Kléber and HSBC on Place Gutenberg.

HEALTH, SAFETY & CRIME

Strasbourg is a safe city to visit and there are no particular health risks. No immunisations or health certificates are required and the tap water is safe to drink.

France has a high standard of medical care. The city's pharmacies can treat minor ailments and display their opening hours in the window.

EU citizens are entitled to free or reduced-cost emergency health care in France with a valid European Health Insurance Card (EHIC), which entitles you to state medical treatment but does not cover repatriation or long-term illness. There is a charge for routine medical care.

Strasbourg has a low crime rate, so you shouldn't experience any problems during your stay. Pickpockets have been known to operate in busy, touristy areas, so it's wise to keep your wits about you and an eye on your wallet. If you are the victim of a crime, you should inform the police by calling 17 (see Emergencies, page 138).

OPENING HOURS

Most shops open 10.00–19.00 Monday to Saturday. A number of shops, cafés and bakeries open on Sundays in the key tourist areas. Banks generally open 08.30–12.30 and 13.30–16.30 Monday to Friday. Some open on Saturdays and many have 24-hour ATMs.

TOILETS

Strasbourg has plenty of clean public toilets. The majority have baby-changing facilities and are accessible for travellers with disabilities. Centrally located toilets include those on Place du Château and Place Kléber (07.00–19.30 Mon–Sat, 08.00–19.30 Sun). You'll find others at Parc de l'Orangerie and Place d'Austerlitz.

CHILDREN

From boat trips along the River Ill to spotting storks at Parc de l'Orangerie, munching on *flammekueche* to visiting interactive science musuems, Strasbourg knows how to keep kids amused.

Home to France's biggest ice rink, more parks than you can shake a stick at and just a stone's throw away from Europa Park, Germany's top theme park, family holidays here spell fun in high doses. The majority of attractions offer a 50 per cent reduction for children and under fives usually go free.

Europa Park A 30-minute drive from Strasbourg, Germany's biggest theme park entertains kids of all ages with everything from the jaw-dropping Pegasus rollercoaster to Atlantica Supersplash. ⓐ Rust ⓣ 01 805 77 66 88 ⓦ www.europapark.de ⓛ 09.00–18.00 Mar–Oct; 11.00–19.00 Dec ⓝ Train: Ringsheim. Admission charge

⬤ *The old rides are the best*

L'Iceberg Glide across France's biggest ice rink in the heart of Strasbourg (see page 35).

Le Vaisseau With its giant climbing frames, creepy crawlies and recording studios, this hands-on museum by the River Ill makes science fun (see page 96).

Théâtre du Jeune Public From circus tricks to puppets and mime, this theatre reels in young audiences (see page 96).

Zoo de l'Orangerie Children can pet animals at the mini farm, spot storks, and come eye-to-eye with lemurs and llamas at the zoo in Parc de l'Orangerie (see page 95).

COMMUNICATIONS
Internet
With its finger on the pulse of the latest technology, Strasbourg has a clutch of central internet cafés offering high-speed, broadband connection. Expect to pay between €2 and €4 for an hour online.

Cyber Café L'Utopie ⓐ 21 rue des Fossé des Tanneurs ⓣ 03 88 23 89 21 ⓦ www.hotel-cyber-21.com ⓛ 06.30–23.30

Net.Sur.Cour ⓐ 18 quai des Pêcheurs ⓣ 03 88 35 66 76 ⓦ www.netsurcour.fr ⓛ 09.30–20.30 Mon–Sat, 14.00–20.00 Sun

Wireless internet access (Wi-Fi) is available in Strasbourg, with numerous hotels, restaurants, bars, cafés and shops in on the act. Among the hotspots of interest to travellers are:

Bar-restaurant Le Cyrano ⓐ 12 rue des Halles

Café Brant ⓐ 11 pl. de l'Université

TELEPHONING FRANCE
Dial 0033 for France, then 3 for Strasbourg plus the eight-digit number.

TELEPHONING ABROAD
To call out of France, simply dial 00 followed by the country code and the local number.

Fnac Strasbourg ⓐ 22 pl. Kléber
Le Pub38 ⓐ 38 rue Wimpheling
Maison Kammerzell ⓐ 16 pl. de la Cathédrale
The Irish Times ⓐ 19 rue Sainte-Barbe

Phone
Very few of Strasbourg's public telephone boxes accept coins, so you'll need to invest in a *télécarte* phonecard, available at most newsagents, supermarkets and post offices. Alternatively you can use your credit card to make calls. The main operator is France Télécom, and the system is reliable and easy to use.
National Directory Enquiries ⓘ 118
International Directory Enquiries ⓘ 3212
Operator ⓘ 3123

Post
You can buy stamps in *tabacs* (newsagents) as well as post offices. Some post offices have ATMs and often a bureau de change. ⓦ www.laposte.fr

ELECTRICITY

France's electricity system is very reliable. It is 220 volts, 50 Hz (round two-pin plugs).

TRAVELLERS WITH DISABILITIES

The majority of attractions and cultural venues are wheelchair accessible, including the Archaeological Museum at the Rohan Palace, the Museum of Modern Art, the National Rhine Opera and Le Vaisseau. Many offer *tarif réduit* (concessions) for visitors with disabilities. Central restaurants with facilities for disabled clients include La Choucrouterie, L'Ancienne Douane, Brasserie au Dauphin and the Art Café.

Australia & New Zealand
Accessibility ⓦ www.accessibility.com.au
Disabled Persons Assembly ⓣ 04 801 9100 ⓦ www.dpa.org.nz

France
Tourisme & Handicaps (National Association for Accessible Tourism) ⓦ www.tourisme-handicaps.org

UK & Ireland
British Council of Disabled People (BCDP) ⓣ 01332 295551
ⓦ www.bcodp.org.uk

USA & Canada
Society for Accessible Travel & Hospitality (SATH)
ⓐ 347 Fifth Ave, New York ⓣ 212 447 7284 ⓦ www.sath.org
Access-Able ⓦ www.access-able.com

TOURIST INFORMATION

Strasbourg Tourist Office Open 365 days a year, Strasbourg's friendly and informative tourist office provides information on attractions, maps, timetables and leaflets, as well as an accommodation and guided tour booking service. You can pick up the Strasbourg Pass here, which is valid for three days and includes museum visits, a boat tour, bike rental and 50 per cent discount on other attractions. ⓐ 17 pl. de la Cathédrale ⓣ 03 88 52 28 28 ⓦ www.ot-strasbourg.fr ⓛ 09.00–19.00

Colmar Tourist Office Colmar's helpful tourist office can provide details on sights and attractions, restaurants, events and where to stay. ⓐ 4 rue Unterlinden ⓣ 03 89 20 68 92 ⓦ www.ot-colmar.fr ⓛ 09.00–19.00 Mon–Sat, 10.00–13.00 Sun, summer; 09.00–12.00, 14.00–18.00 Mon–Sat, 10.00–13.00 Sun, winter

Saverne Tourist Office Pick up maps, browse leaflets and book accommodation at Saverne's helpful visitor centre. ⓐ 37 Grand Rue ⓣ 03 88 91 80 47 ⓦ www.ot-saverne.fr ⓛ 09.30–12.00, 14.00–18.00 Mon–Sat, 10.00–12.00, 14.00–17.00 Sun, May–Sept & Dec; 10.00–12.00, 14.00–18.00 Mon–Sat, Jan–Apr & Oct

Alsace Tourism This site gives the lowdown on the Alsace region, from history to heritage sights, nature reserves, wine and travel. ⓦ www.tourisme-alsace.com

French National Tourist Office Everything you ever wanted to know about travel in France can be found on this comprehensive website. ⓦ www.franceguide.com

BACKGROUND READING

Images of Alsace by Della Meyers, Kiera Tchelistcheff, Frederic Engel. This wonderfully illustrated book will get you excited about travelling to Strasbourg and Alsace, covering themes such as architecture, tradition, nature and gastronomy.

Talk to the Snail by Stephen Clarke. A hilarious guide on getting to grips with the French language, culture and quirks. This is essential holiday reading for Francophiles.

The Wines of Alsace by Tom Stevenson. If you're into wine, the pages of this book take you on a tour of Alsace's vineyards and whet your appetite to taste the grape.

● *A stork welcomes you to Strasbourg's tourist office*

Emergencies

Emergency services ℹ 112
Police ℹ 17
Fire & ambulance ℹ 18
SAMU (paramedic) ℹ 15

ℹ When you dial the European emergency number 112, ask for the service you require. The operator will connect you to the service you need.

ℹ You may spot *gendarmes* (police officers) patrolling the streets while in Strasbourg; they wear navy blue uniforms. If you need to contact the main station, dial ☎ 03 90 23 17 17.

MEDICAL SERVICES

It is strongly recommended to have a valid health insurance policy before travelling to France even if you are covered for emergency health care by the European Health Insurance Card (see page 131). In case of accident or illness, emergency pharmacists can be reached by calling ☎ 03 88 41 11 34.

ℹ The centrally located civil hospital provides emergency medical care. ⓐ Pl. de l'Hôpital Civil ☎ 03 88 11 67 68
ⓦ www.chru-strasbourg.fr

EMBASSIES, CONSULATES & COUNCILS

Australian ⓐ 4 rue Jean Rey, Paris ☎ 01 40 59 33 00
ⓦ www.france.embassy.gov.au 🕒 09.00–17.00 Mon–Fri
Canadian ⓐ 35 av. Montaigne, Paris ☎ 01 44 43 29 00
ⓦ www.amb-canada.fr 🕒 09.00–12.00, 14.00–17.00 Mon–Fri

EMERGENCY PHRASES

Help!	**Fire!**	**Stop!**
Au secours!	Au feu!	Stop!
Ossercoor!	*Oh fur!*	*Stop!*

Call an ambulance/a doctor/the police/the fire service!
Appelez une ambulance/un médecin/la police/les pompiers!
*Ahperleh ewn ahngbewlahngss/ang medesang/lah poleess/
leh pompeeyeh!*

Council of Europe @ Av. de l'Europe, Strasbourg ☏ 03 88 41 20 00
🔘 www.coe.int
Republic of Ireland @ 12 av. Foch, Paris ☏ 1 44 17 67 00
🕒 09.30–13.00, 14.30–17.30 Mon–Fri
Irish Representative to the Council of Europe:
@ 15 av. de la Liberté, Strasbourg ☏ 03 88 14 49 20 1
South African @ 59 quai d'Orsay, Paris ☏ 01 53 59 23 23
🔘 www.afriquesud.net 🕒 08.30–17.15 Mon–Fri
UK @ 18 bis rue d'Anjou, Paris ☏ 01 44 51 31 00
🔘 www.britishembassy.gov.uk 🕒 09.30–12.30, 14.30–16.30 Mon–Fri
US @ 2 av. Gabriel, Paris ☏ 01 43 12 22 22
🔘 http://france.usembassy.gov 🕒 09.00–13.00,
14.00–17.00 Mon–Fri
American Consulate General @ 15 av. d'Alsace, Strasbourg
☏ 03 88 35 31 04 🔘 http://france.usembassy.gov
🕒 09.00–17.00 Mon–Fri

A

accommodation 37–41,
    114–15, 125–6
air travel 50, 128
arts see culture
ATMs 130

B

background reading 137
banks 130
Barrage Vauban 76
bars, clubs & pubs
    see nightlife
Bartholdi,
    Frédéric Auguste 110
boat travel 64, 108–9
bridges 80
bureaux de change 130
bus travel 51, 58, 129

C

Cabinet des Estampes
    et des Dessins 64–6
cafés 48–49, 71–2, 83–86,
    98–100, 112–13, 123
Cagliostro, Count 119–20
campsites 41, 125–6
canoeing 35
car hire 58
Cathédrale de
    Notre-Dame 60
Cave des
    Hospices Civils 81
Centre Tomi Ungerer 66
Château de Haut Barr 118

Château du
    Greifenstein 117
Château Rohan
    (Saverne) 120
children 10–11, 14, 95,
    96–7, 131–3
Christmas festivities 13,
    14–15
city centre 60–75
Cloître des Récollets 118
Collégiale
    Saint-Martin 105
Colmar 104–15, 136
consulates 138–9
Council of Europe 139
crime 54, 131
culture 20–2, 33–4,
    46–7, 48
customs & duty 130
cycling 36, 55, 122

D

disabilities 135
driving 54, 58, 105, 110,
    117, 129

E

Église des
    Dominicains 105
Église St Thomas 77
electricity 135
embassies 138–9
emergencies 138–9
entertainment 31–4
    see also nightlife
Europa Park 132

European
    organisations 17, 139
events 10–13, 14–15, 46–7

F

festivals 10–13, 14–15,
    46–7
foie gras 24, 26, 29, 70,
    111–12, 123
food & drink 27–30,
    48–9, 110
football 35

G

Goethe, Johann
    Wolfgang von 19, 81, 94
Grand Ile 60–75

H

health 130–1, 138
history 16–17
hostels 41, 114, 125
hotels 37–41, 126

I

ice skating 35, 133
Ill river 64, 80
insurance 130–1, 138
internet 133–4

J

Jardin Botanique
    (Saverne) 118
Jardin Botanique
    (Strasbourg) 90

K

Krutenau & University
    District 90–102

L

L'Horloge
  Astronomique 64
La Choucrouterie 81–2
La Laiterie 22
language 18–19, 26, 30,
  55, 139
Le Chalet 33
Le Meinau stadium 35
Le Vaisseau 96–7, 139
lifestyle 18–19, 54
listings 31, 34

M

Maison Kammerzell 64
Maison Martin
  Jund 105–8
Maison Pfister 108
Maison St-Florent 120
Maison des Têtes 108
malls 25–6, 70
markets 14, 26, 27–8,
  70, 123
money 130
Musée Alsacien 66
Musée Archéologique 67
Musée d'Art Moderne
  et Contemporain 82
Musée des Arts
  Décoratifs 67
Musée Bartholdi 110
Musée d'Histoire
  Naturelle et
  d'Ethnographie 110–111

Musée de l'Oeuvre
  Notre-Dame 66
Musée d'Unterlinden 111
Musée Zoologique 96
music 11–13, 15, 20–2,
  31–4, 46–7

N

Naviscope Alsace 96
nightlife 31–4, 74–5,
  88–9, 102

O

opening hours 24, 130, 131
Opéra National
  du Rhin 66–7

P

Palais de la Musique
  et des Congrès 22
Palais Rohan
  (Strasbourg) 67
Parc de la Citadelle 91
Parc de l'Orangerie 94
parks & green spaces 46,
  90, 91, 94–5, 118, 119
passports & visas 129
Petite France 76–89
Petite Venise 108–9
phones 134
picnics 28
Place de l'Ancienne
  Douane 109
Place de la Licorne 118–19
Place de l'Université 94
Planetarium 94–95

police 131, 138
Ponts Couverts 80
post 134
public holidays 13
public transport 50–1,
  55–8, 105, 117, 128–9

Q

Quai de la
  Petite France 81

R

rail travel 50–1, 105, 117,
  128–9
restaurants 27, 30, 72–4,
  86–8, 100–2, 113–14, 125
Roseraie 119
Route des Vins
  d'Alsace 110

S

safety 54, 130–1
Saut du Prince Charles 119
Saverne 116–26, 136
seasons 10
shopping 14, 24–6, 48,
  67–70, 83, 98, 111–12,
  122–3
spa 36, 120–2
sport & activities 35–6,
  120–2
Strasbourg Pass 136
storks 97
swimming 35–6, 120–2
symbols &
  abbreviations 6

T

theatre 22, 67, 81–2, 97
Théâtre du Jeune
  Public 96, 133
Théâtre National
  de Strasbourg 67
theme park 132
time difference 50
tipping 30
toilets 131
Tour Cagliostro 119–20

tourist information 136–7
tours 64
tram travel 58

U

Ungerer, Tomi 66
unicorns 118–19
University of
  Strasbourg 19, 94

W

walking & hiking 36, 46,
  55, 122

water sports 35–6
weather 10, 48–9
wine 29–30, 81, 98,
  105–8, 110
winstubs 27, 73, 86, 88,
  100–1, 110

Z

Zoo de l'Orangerie 95, 133

SPOTTED YOUR NEXT CITY BREAK?

...then these lightweight CitySpots pocket guides will have you in the know in no time, wherever you're heading.

Covering over 90 cities worldwide, they're packed with detail on the most important urban attractions from shopping and sights to non-stop nightlife; knocking spots off chunkier, clunkier versions.

Aarhus
Amsterdam
Antwerp
Athens
Bangkok
Barcelona
Belfast
Belgrade
Berlin
Biarritz
Bilbao
Bologna
Bordeaux
Bratislava
Bruges
Brussels
Bucharest
Budapest
Cairo
Cape Town
Cardiff
Cologne
Copenhagen
Cork
Dubai
Dublin
Dubrovnik
Düsseldorf
Edinburgh
Fez
Florence
Frankfurt

Gdansk
Geneva
Genoa
Glasgow
Gothenburg
Granada
Hamburg
Hanover
Helsinki
Hong Kong
Istanbul
Kiev
Krakow
Kuala Lumpur
Leipzig
Lille
Lisbon
Liverpool
Ljubljana
London
Los Angeles
Lyon
Madrid
Marrakech
Marseilles
Milan
Monte Carlo
Moscow
Munich
Naples
New York City
Nice

Oslo
Palermo
Palma
Paris
Pisa
Prague
Porto
Reykjavik
Riga
Rome
Rotterdam
Salzburg
Sarajevo
Seville
Singapore
Sofia
Stockholm
Strasbourg
St Petersburg
Tallinn
Tirana
Tokyo
Toulouse
Turin
Valencia
Venice
Verona
Vienna
Vilnius
Warsaw
Zagreb
Zurich

Available from all good bookshops, your local Thomas Cook travel store or browse and buy online at www.thomascookpublishing.com

Thomas Cook Publishing

Editorial/project management: Lisa Plumridge
Copy editor: Paul Hines
Layout/DTP: Alison Rayner

The publishers would like to thank the following individuals and organisations for supplying their copyright photographs for this book: Andy Christiani, pages 1, 7, 23, 47, 49, 85, 99, 104 & 115; Hôtel Hannong, page 40; Hôtel Kléber, page 39; Stanley Rippel/ Dreamstime.com, page 61; World Pictures, page 15; Jonathan Smith, all others.

The author would like to thank Andy Christiani for his help in researching this guide.

Send your thoughts to
books@thomascook.com

- **Found a great bar, club, shop or must-see sight that we don't feature**.
- **Like to tip us off about any information that needs a little updating?**
- **Want to tell us what you love about this handy little guidebook and more importantly how we can make it even handier?**

Then here's your chance to tell all! Send us ideas, discoveries and recommendations today and then look out for your valuable input in the next edition of this title.

Email the above address (stating the title) or write to: CitySpots Series Editor, Thomas Cook Publishing, PO Box 227, Coningsby Road, Peterborough PE3 8SB, UK.